ON ACTIVE SERVICE
IN WAR AND PEACE

POLITICS AND IDEOLOGY
IN THE AMERICAN
HISTORICAL PROFESSION

by Jesse Lemisch

with an introduction
by Thomas Schofield

NEW HOGTOWN PRESS
TORONTO
1975

This essay was originally entitled "Present-Mindedness Revisited: Anti-Radicalism as a Goal of American Historical Writing Since World War II."

copyright © 1969, 1975 Jesse Lemisch

Introduction copyright © 1975 Thomas Schofield

ISBN Number 0-919940-00-5

Library of Congress Catalogue Card Number 75-18557

Canadian Shared Cataloguing in Publication Data

Lemisch, Jesse
On active service in war and peace: politics and ideology in the American historical profession/Jesse Lemisch; with an introd. by Thomas Schofield.

1. United States — Historiography. 2. Historians — United States. 3. Radicalism.
I. Title.

E175.L35 973.07'2073

typeset by Better Read Typesetting

layout by volunteer labour

cover design by Barry Sampson © 1975

"Although it is written in the third person, th[is] book has no other aim than to present the record of Mr. Stimson's public life as he himself sees it. It is an attempt to substitute a joint effort for the singlehanded autobiography he might have undertaken if he were a little younger. It follows that we have made no effort at an external assessment, and in the writing I have sought not to intrude any views of my own, but rather to present Mr. Stimson's actions as he himself understands them. Thus objective praise and blame are equally absent. . . .

The major sources of the book are two: Mr. Stimson himself and his records. If I have held the labouring oar, Mr. Stimson has held the tiller rope, and the judgments and opinions expressed are always his. . . .

In every important sense, then, this is Mr. Stimson's book."

> McGeorge Bundy, "A Note of Explanation and Acknowledgment," in Henry L. Stimson and McGeorge Bundy, *On Active Service in Peace and War* (New York, 1948), 673, 676

"So vast indeed is the set of connections which now bind the world of power and the world of learning that it is a matter of the greatest difficulty to isolate particular parts of the connection for close analysis.

. . . I believe there are great opportunities for a much wider and stronger connection between universities and governments than we yet have. . . . What there is not enough of yet, and what I come to praise, is the kind of academic work which proceeds from the same centre of concern as that of the man who is himself committed to an active part in government. That centre of concern is the taking and use of power itself.

For this kind of work I find no better word than history."

McGeorge Bundy, "The Battlefields of Power and the Searchlights of the Academy," in E.A.J. Johnson, ed., *The Dimensions of Diplomacy* (Baltimore, 1964), 1, 8-9

PREFACE

*On Active Service In War And Peace,** by Jesse Lemisch, was originally presented in condensed form under the title "Present-Mindedness Revisited: Anti-Radicalism as a Goal of American Historical Writing Since World War II," at the December 1969 meeting of the American Historical Association in Washington, D.C. It received an enthusiastic response at the time. Subsequent media attention and word of mouth produced a heavy demand for the paper.** Then, and in the years since, Lemisch has responded to the requests by sending out photocopies. But the demand has remained high, and so he has consented to let New Hogtown Press print it in its original form in order to make it more easily available to those who continue to ask for it and others who may find it useful.

Lemisch responds to New Hogtown's initiative with reluctance, since he feels the paper has problems and should be revised, but other work prevents him from doing so. Under these circumstances, he feels it would be ahistorical for him to do what he describes as "some quick protective word-changing which would have the effect of making me look retroactively better." The paper expresses the way he saw and put things in 1969; and so we print it precisely as in

---

* Lemisch calls to mind the total surrender of the scholar's independence in the explicitly and militantly uncritical attitude taken by an establishment scholar toward his establishment subject: Henry L. Stimson and McGeorge Bundy, *On Active Service in Peace and War* (New York: Harper and Bros., 1948). See, for instance, Bundy's justification of the World War II internment of Americans of Japanese descent (p. 406). [After earlier stints as Secretary of War and Secretary of State Stimson was Roosevelt's Secretary of War 1940-1945. Bundy has progressed Harvard to the Kennedy Administration to the Ford Foundation.]

** See: *New York Times,* Dec. 29, 1969; Jan. 15, 1970; [Joseph

the original. But clearly, as is indicated in the Introduction, he would do differently in 1975 what was originally done in 1969.

Although "Present-Mindedness Revisited" was written for delivery at the 1969 meeting of the American Historical Association, it was also intended as an intial treatment and framework for a collaborative work with Christopher Z. Hobson, which was then being planned. The subject of the work was to be "academic origins of the ideology of repression": liberal academic ideologies in the cold war period and since, with special attention to the universities and repression. As planned, the work would have contained extensive material on the historical profession, framed by a more general discussion of liberal academic ideology and conduct. This collaborative work was never completed. Starting from the historical sections of "Present-Mindedness Revisited," Lemisch researched and drafted an extended critical study of the history of the concept of social utility in the historical profession, from the late nineteenth century to the post-World War II period. But the material was immense, and as the manuscript expanded, so did the work which would have been necessary to put it in final shape. Wanting instead to return to his primary scholarly commitment—American history seen "from the bottom up," especially in the Colonial and Revolutionary periods—Lemisch withdrew from the collaboration. Meanwhile, during the collaborative phase, Hobson had used the

Featherstone], "Scholars and Society," *New Republic*, Jan. 17, 1970, pp. 7-8; Ronald Radosh, "Annual Set-to: The Bare-Knuckled Historians," *The Nation*, Feb. 2, 1970, reprinted in Blanche W. Cook, Alice K. Harris, Ronald Radosh, eds., *Past Imperfect: Alternative Essays in American History* (New York: Alfred Knopf, 1973) II, pp. 339-41; Clifford Solway, "Turning History Upside Down," *Saturday Review*, June 20, 1970, pp. 13-15, 62-64.

non-historical sections of "Present-Mindedness Revisited" as his framework, but had done extensive additional work. After Lemisch's withdrawal, Hobson continued on his own and went beyond the framework of the collaboration; he added much, both in the way of new material and new interpretations, and ultimately produced a manuscript which incorporates parts of "Present-Mindedness Revisited" but goes beyond it, standing on its own under the title *The Ideology of Repression*. When Hobson's book is published, we will have a monumental and detailed study of the role of liberal intellectuals and the universities in the period since World War II.

New Hogtown Press
May, 1975

TABLE OF CONTENTS

INTRODUCTION *

Jesse Lemisch's essay, *On Active Service in War and Peace*, is the most complete account yet written on the politics of American historians. It is a carefully documented, explosive condemnation of the writing of U.S. history.

Since it was written in the late 1960s, the Lemisch paper has acquired a political history of its own. Its history indicates the importance of what Lemisch has uncovered and demonstrates the difficulties that beset the scholar who attempts to uncover the secret history that the mainstream of the profession chooses to leave untold. The paper also has a continuing significance for those interested in the history of repression in academic life. It speaks directly to the situation in the United States, exposing the creation of a national history the themes of which have often been governed by political bias. That bias, and the repression which has blatantly attempted to close the historical profession to radicals and Marxists, did not abate with the Lemisch exposé in 1969, or with the subsequent becalming of the student and anti-war movements. Canadians would be well advised to consider seriously the themes that Lemisch presents: while the Canadian historical profession is considerably smaller than the American, it will be demonstrated that many Canadian historians, like their American colleagues, have pursued a political course overtly committed to anti-radicalism. Widespread repression has continued to the present time on both sides of the 49th parallel.

* Thomas Schofield received his Honours BA in Modern History and English from the University of Toronto in 1971. He has completed graduate study in Law and History at the State University of New York at Buffalo.

I.

In 1969 the American Historical Association held its convention in Washington, D.C. The war in Southeast Asia was still the central political concern of the American people. The convention faced the first major attempts of liberals and radicals to raise the issue of Viet Nam within the profession. An avowedly radical group of historians confronted establishment scholars, creating a marked contrast from the aura of gentility and decorum which traditionally characterized meetings of the Association. The Radical Caucus presented a resolution to the Business Meeting condemning the war in Viet Nam; this failed, as did a more liberal version. Radicals also challenged a tradition within the profession of election without contest by audaciously running a slate of counter-candidates for Association offices. Participatory democracy emerged as an alternative to the establishment politics of the Official Nominating Board. While showing some strength, the counter-candidates lost. The Movement within the profession had thrown its energies into a host of issues and had successively followed a broad variety of strategies. But it emerged from the process somewhat shaken and uncertain of its role and purpose.

Perhaps fittingly in the context of a learned society, radical scholarship fared better than radical politics. Discussing the role of radicals at the Convention in *The Nation*, left historian Ronald Radosh came close to despair. However, the significant impact of Lemisch's paper stood out in sharp contrast with less successful radical efforts, and Radosh concluded:

> Perhaps defeat was averted by a paper delivered on the final convention day by Jesse Lemisch, a historian who had been dismissed from the University of Chicago because his "political concerns interfered with his scholarship." In what may

be the most telling and fundamental critique presented before the AHA he proposed that the supposedly unpolitical stars of the profession (Allan Nevins, Arthur M. Schlesinger Jr., Samuel Eliot Morison, Oscar Handlin, Daniel Boorstin and others) were implicit cold warriors who sought to use history as a vehicle in the fight against communism. Lemisch's paper. . . argued persuasively that what so many object to is not that a scholar should take a political position but that he should hold views contrary to establishment shibboleths.[1]

The Lemisch presentation was an electric moment for a large part of the American historical profession. He had publicly declared what many knew to be the case, but until that moment, the charges of anti-radicalism had not been supported by systematic documentation. The subsequent history is more sobering. A *New York Times* account of the Lemisch speech foresaw the typical reaction the paper would receive by treating it as an isolated phenomenon. Failing to note that Lemisch spoke for a significant minority of historians the *Times* report treated the Lemisch presentation as a threat, devoting itself to Lemisch's own conclusion: "Fire us, expel us, jail us. We will not go away."[2]

Lemisch was not exactly threatening the profession; he was presenting them with data. But the historians, to a large degree, simply excluded his findings from circulation or serious consideration. It is not an accident that the manuscript has remained largely underground, surfacing now only through the efforts of a left publisher. The paper's history is an example of the working of repression. It suggests that radicals have spoken but found the communicative organs of the profession hostile to the radical voice.

When this text was submitted to the *American Historical Review* editor R.K. Webb rejected it. Acknowledging that his letter might seem "singularly rude and condescending," Webb nonetheless noted that Lemisch had "unjustly" convicted "a good many of my close friends" of "historical derelictions." Webb was convinced that Lemisch's charges could be more accurately explained, not as a systematic critique of the profession but as "indiscretions or lapses or outrageous gaffes by some." He accused Lemisch of seeing an "anti-radical conspiracy." One particularly open call for Cold War activism, mentioned in the Lemisch text, was a plea by Conyers Read that American historians participate "in what everyone is calling education for democracy." Read urged the supression of data while advocating "social control" as a weapon in the Cold War. Referring to Lemisch's condemnation of this appeal, and of the silence with which Read's speech was greeted, Webb asked Lemisch: "Has it occurred to you to ask how many people who heard Conyers Read's presidential address must have cringed with horror?"[3]

Webb maintained that his remarks were not the product of "some prejudice excited by your attack." However, while Lemisch's critique of the profession was being dismissed as a series of random examples, the rejection of Lemisch's text was occasion for reflection by Webb upon the state of New Left scholarship in general:

> . . . I wonder if the activism of the New Left historians today, unlike the activism you so deplore in your article, may not be a bar to serious scholarship that can appeal to any scholar outside the sect itself.[4]

The response was similar when the paper was submitted to the *Journal of American History*, the major scholarly journal for the publication of articles on United States history. Martin Ridge, the editor, wrote back that the "essay more than any I have read in several years has disturbed me."[5] He advised Lemisch to go and read the story of Diego Rivera, the Mexican communist painter,[6] who included the head of Lenin among the portraits presented in a mural painted in 1933 in the Rockefeller Center. Young Nelson Rockefeller wrote the artist a letter asking that he "substitute the face of some unknown man where Lenin's face now appears."[7] Rivera refused, and Rockefeller had the mural destroyed. The episode became the subject of a famous poem "I Paint What I See" by E.B. White. The message intended for Lemisch was clear: the *Journal,* like the Rockefeller Center, was not a proper medium for expressing a certain point of view.

An outside reader, who commented on the Lemisch submission for the *Journal,* told Ridge:

> I don't know how you can tell him that he simply cannot do this, and that he certainly cannot do it in the pages of the *Journal.* He probably believes that he can, which says something about how far he and his ilk are estranged from civilization.[8]

This rejection, like the other one, was accompanied by phrases about keeping the profession open to all points of view and by promises that real scholarship would be warmly received.

Other criticisms were equally direct. John Higham, who had earlier raised questions about the sterility of consensus history, rejected Lemisch's solicitation of his comments: "I am afraid that I am not enough in sympathy with the spirit of your paper to have comments that might be useful to you." From Higham's perspective, Lemisch's work threatened good relations between radical students and members of the profession; emphasis upon "alleged derelictions of behavior" limits the possibility for rational discourse by lessening respect for good intentions.[9]

Many of the historians criticized by Lemisch were still active in the profession. Students were exposed to their questionable work on a daily basis. To argue that Lemisch's work would create hostility was equivalent to asserting that intellectual problems are the work of outside agitators. In fact, many radical students were challenging their teachers and their careers suffered on account of it. What the Lemisch paper would most effectively do was collate the documentation, so authority could be brought to both sides of the argument. It would no longer be so easy to assert that New Left scholars were political and the mainstream free from bias.

II.

The general reasons, indeed the necessity, for bringing Lemisch's research on anti-radicalism among U.S. historians to a wider audience follow directly from continued hostility to radicalism.

On the whole, the text has aged well. Much of his discussion of the historians' role in legitimizing "executive usurpation" is directly relevant to Watergate. Moreover, the tone of the 1960s must seem less strident to many who thought it so at the time, and more nearly a sane response to those years—both within the profession and in national politics in the U.S. Where the language is angry, it sets the historical place of the piece and is a reminder of why this had to be written and why it was not well received by the historical establishment. The justification for the hardened attack is based upon crucial concepts. What Lemisch uncovers is in fact serious business, and the instances of anti-radicalism he finds are not individual lapses or indiscretions as they have been characterized by defenders of the mainstream of the historical profession.

Nonetheless, after reading the above barrage of criticisms, it is fair to ask whether all is political or whether there are problems of substance which mar the text. In conversations with this writer Lemisch has pointed to various flaws and has especially stressed certain points which he would have dealt with at length had he been able to undertake revision.

Lemisch acknowledges that there were many other historians—whom he did not mention—who do not fit the pattern he described; but the trend he describes must be seen as the *dominant* one in the absence of evidence for any other single competing trend with equal influence. Lemisch presented abundant evidence of such a dominant trend. Those who would challenge him must produce evidence of an equally strong counter trend. R.K. Webb's vision of historians "cringing with horror" is inadequate evidence of such opposition (unless historians are truly inarticulate). The characterization of the damning passages as mere individual lapses is in fact additional evidence of anti-radical bias.

Similarly, the charges that Lemisch is strident, shrill, excessive and even hysterical are illustrative of a political stereotype familar in American society (especially to Blacks and women among others). That which reflects acceptable values is spirited, while that which offends is rabid, emotional, or off the wall. An establishment that frequently conducts itself with minimal good manners requires civility only of those with whom it disagrees.

On the other hand, Lemisch does see some accuracy in the criticism that he grouped together a wide range of historians without adequate attention to the differences among them. For example, the liberal activism of Arthur Schlesinger Jr. can be distinguished from the conservative activism of an historian like Daniel J. Boorstin. Lemisch concedes that there are significant differences among the historians he dealt with and that a more sophisticated approach would develop these differences to advantage.

It is also true, but largely unnoticed, that such distinctions are not central to Lemisch's argument. Liberals and conservatives may have their differences, but on the question of anti-radicalism in the profession they are in general agreement. In fact, Boorstin's dinner engagements at the White House suggest that their differences on the general question of activism may be explained by a simple analysis of who holds the reins of power.[10] In any case the alliance is strong. And when liberals or conservatives speak of openness or pluralism within the profession they share a common definition, an acceptance of known outer limits, marking the range of the permissible. Within that context, elucidation of the differences between historians like Daniel J. Boorstin and Arthur Schlesinger Jr. would obscure important truths. Acknowledging the real differences among the historians treated does not lead to the simplistic pluralist conclusion that they are just a diverse and cantankerous lot without common ideological bonds. They share a common ideology: they are hostile to radicalism, and they impose that hostility on the past.[11]

The more liberal activists of the historical profession may not have openly espoused the dogma of their more conservative counterparts. But there is a sense in which subtle differences make little difference. Liberals who defended free speech, while attacking Marxists for abusing its limits, provided potent ammunition for the conservatives who demanded censorship and supression. Both were threatening the Left, and each position was a reinforcement of the other. Lemisch's data demonstrates that historians and university intellectuals were in the forefront of the anti-radical hysteria of the 1950s. Moreover, they continued that role in the attack on the New Left that emerged in the later

1960s. The liberals have deliberately chosen to ignore what E.P. Thompson has called the "sociology of presentation". In an extended discussion of the workings of liberal anti-radicalism, Thompson points to the manner in which criticism of the Left is used and circulated. Past practice guarantees that remarks presented in certain forums will be used out of context in an attempt to discredit and destroy the Left. Hence the subsequent distribution and use of criticism must be considered in the original presentation of a critique. Thompson explained:

> If you criticise with stridency, any section of the Left in certain places . . . your criticism is not attended to for the sake of any particular discrimination which it may contain. It is absorbed, instantly, into ideology; that is, it is simply assimilated as one more *noise* against the Left, one more evidence that *all* the Left has failed,is brutal, *all* Marxism is incoherent etc. . . . [I]t is a veritable trophy to be hung at the cloudy altar of the established gods.[12]

This is as true in judgements of the past as it is in discussion of present events. And it is not a fact of extraordinary subtlety: the more liberal of the anti-radical academics have found themselves holding hands with their more conservative brethren.

Some readers and listeners took "Present-Mindedness Revisited" as an exhortation to desert the ideal of scholarly objectivity. As the *New Republic* put it: Lemisch's rebuke against establishment activists was "well-deserved, although it was never entirely clear whether Mr. Lemisch was finding his enemies wanting by the standard of neutrality, or whether he was repudiating the standard altogether."[13] Although the essay exposes the extent to which "mainstream" historians have used their history as a vehicle for expressing their political commitments, it hardly constitutes a call for radicals to emulate them. Actually, Lemisch believes that historians of all political persuasions should become more aware of their biases.[14] He has rejected "relevance" as a primary goal while clinging to a belief in the importance of striving for objective validity in history.

This position has it problems. The demand for relevance in the late 1960s was political. Scholarship, which largely existed in service of the status quo, could be used also in the attempt to change the world. In practice, the standards of truth were often battered in the attempt to get to the part where the world changed. Whatever social change can be wrought by service to a relevance in which truth is obscured or ignored can only be accidentally progressive, and will more likely be regressive or insignificant. To this writer, Lemisch creates a false dichotomy. Relevance is not an obstacle to objective inquiry. Rather it is dubious that it can be avoided. Its presence pervades the historical process and its force must be recognized rather than wished away. It appears at the outset in the choice of subject matter as the first object to which such inquiry must be applied. And subsequently, questions of relevance influence every aspect of the research: what data, what questions do we ask of the data, how much data, and what interpretive results are indicated from the evidence uncovered? That many writers have sacrificed their objectivity in the service of relevance is a *non sequitur;* evidence pointing to a danger, but not a necessary result.[15]

(Right or wrong, Lemisch's stance is illustrated in the titles of some of his other writings. In another session on "radical history" at the 1969 AHA meeting he presented a paper entitled: " 'What's Your Evidence?' Radical Scholarship as Scientific Method and Anti-Authoritarianism, not 'Relevance'." Earlier, at a founding meeting of the New University Conference he had written "Who Will Write a

Left History of Art While We are all Putting Our Balls on the Line?"[16])

One final comment should be made to put this paper in the context of its time and place. "Present-Mindedness Revisited" was an attack on establishment history and historians, and, as such did not reflect Lemisch's critical view of certain trends emerging on the Left at that time. For a critique of elitism, authoritarianism, and male chauvinism within the "movement", and a defence of "rationalism", see Lemisch, " 'If You Gotta Ask, Man, You'll Never Know'."[17]

III.

"From the extreme left there have been few contributions to Canadian historiography," wrote Robin Winks of Yale in 1966, "for Canadian scholars reflect their nation is being essentially liberal-conservatives." Citing deficiencies in the writing of Canadian history, Winks focused upon the lack of an adequate study of the "national parks system."[18] Canadian historians have often denounced Marxism and dismissed the importance of radical historical interpretation; Winks' comments are part of the mainstream tradition. Among those who have expressed sentiments hostile to radicals are A.R.M. Lower, Donald Grant Creighton, Hilda Neatby, Gad Horowitz, Frank Underhill, H.N. Fieldhouse, and John Bartlet Brebner. As a group, they span almost the entire range of "legitimate" political opinion in Canada. No matter what their disagreements in other areas, generations of Canadian historians have shared values hostile to radicalism. Within this almost universal agreement, the insignificance of radical alternatives has been taken as a given, something that need not be proved.

A.R.M. Lower advised his readers that "doctrinaire ideas, such as Marxism, have had little influence in Canada except negatively, by way of delaying the logical evolution of industrial society."[19] Creighton declared "Canadian history was a sadly imperfect vehicle for the exemplification of the Marxian verities."[20] Neatby wrote disparagingly of the "Marxian myth of the class struggle."[21] Gad Horowitz observed that Canadians "do not speak the same language" as "other worldly" Marxists.[22] He pointed out that communists, like catholics and fascists, "relate to the world in a paranoid manner."[23] J.B. Brebner speculated that it was "quite tempting" to take the "developments of Canada and the United States as examples for the refutation of a Marxian or economic interpretation of history."[24] Fieldhouse argued that "we have never known . . . a Left exclusively anti-christian or proletarian".[25] Underhill began his search for the Canadian identity with the conclusion that the Left was weak in Canada. He dismissed the *significance* of radicalism (owing to the lack of an eighteenth century), then failed to mention its *existence* at any subsequent point in his discussion. Liberalism was affirmed as essential to the fabric of Canadian society.[26] Each of these assertions points toward two truths: the weakness of a Left or Marxist example in the writing of Canadian history and an inherent anti-radicalism on the part of a great many of the traditional historians. The Left largely failed to rebut the assertions presented by the mainstream, but one might still test the evidence upon which those conclusions were made. The resulting answer must inevitably be: a combination of faith and establishment politics.

Many historians refused to seriously consider a Marxist interpretation when it was offered. Stanley Ryerson was for years unable to get a teaching position; his books were published on the Left but were excluded from reading lists, omitted from the content of university curricula, and belittled by reviewers.[27] The hostility with which Ryerson was dismissed is typified by Gustave Lanctot's short review of *The Founding of Canada* in the *Canadian Historical Review*. Characterizing the book as "predetermined and predictive all the way to the last line," he asserted that Ryerson's conclusion was "automatic." Lanctot quickly dismissed the idea of the "people's exploitation by the ruling class" as "undocumented assertion," despite Ryerson's "extensive information." Ryerson "missed a fine opportunity to pen a more detached story of Canada's march to democracy."[28]

Present day events, especially the early days of World War II and the Cold War, triggered the worst of the anti-radical excesses of Canadian historians. When the Cold War emerged in Canada, it did so largely in the guise of fundamental American political positions. Underhill boldly declared the "self evident truth" that "some effective form of North Atlantic alliance is essential for the preservation of our western civilization."[29] Liberals looked to the United States to spearhead that alliance; conservatives were less certain that historic British leadership should be dispossessed.

But even Canadians who questioned the northward export of Cold War ideology were inclined to accept the truth of its basic premises; they sought a Canadian contribution that would be distinctive while supporting the general position of the "Western World." In a 1954 essay, "Canada and the Cold War," Donald Grant Creighton eyed the Cold War political situation from a critical northern perspective:

> In other matters, in which we are much less directly concerned, Canadians are even more disposed to accept the latest advice from Washington as the modern equivalent of divine revelation. For the past eight years the nation which

virtually invented modern advertising has been engaged in what can only be described as the greatest sales campaign in history, the campaign to sell the Cold War in an exclusive American package, to the rest of the Western world. Canada, which was treated as an adjunct of the domestic market, received the full impact of this promotion. To put it in commercial terms, which are in reality most appropriate, American packaged Cold War was outselling every other brand of packaged Cold War ten to one in the Canadian market. The policies and opinions of other Western countries were given prominence chiefly when they agreed with those of the United States; and the contradictory decisions or views of such countries as Great Britain, France of India were depicted as unsound, mischievous, doubtfully loyal, or Communist-inspired.[30]

Creighton was partly correct in his observations of Cold War culture. Nonetheless, his bias left many of the important questions unanswered: why the particular receptivity of the Canadian "market" for an ideology Creighton sought to characterize as "foreign"? Who ultimately produced the package and how was it perceived in different segments of society? Creighton's fellow historians were particularly enamoured with the politics of the Cold War; Creighton was projecting their enthusiasm upon other classes in Canada.

Creighton was, in fact, opposed to the American ideology he described. But his opposition was not sustained by a more modern or humane set of principles. He believed in the virtues of government under the old constitutional monarchy and he rejected both bourgeois republicanism and socialist formulations of government and society. Both were revolutionary in origin, and "the simple truth was that the revolutionary tradition was completely incompatible with Canada's historic position in the external world."[31]

Creighton developed this theme fully in his Presidential

Address to the Canadian Historical Association in 1957. Reviewing the historical writing of the previous twenth-five years, Creighton focused his attack upon the "Liberal interpretation of Canadian history."[32] Like the American Cold War package, it too took on "something of the awful grandeur of divine relevation."[33] Creighton tied the practitioners of the liberal interpretation to the Liberal government in power: "the professional scribes of the Authorized Version were called to Ottawa."[34] Creighton rejected one political view on the grounds that politics were incompatible with "the careful and imaginative study of the facts of Canadian history." But he also articulated a political position of his own; "the Marxian economic interpretation of history" was adopted by "victims of superior propaganda" who accepted a "doctrine which was alien to their experience and unremunerative for their purposes."[35]

Creighton offered no evidence to support his own political pronouncements, but he lectured his fellow historians as to the limits of modern political options:

> How wrong we were! How imitative, how gullible, how truly colonially-minded! Only now has it become possible for us to realize the enormous extent of our deception. The War and the twelve years that have elapsed since its conclusion have ended our dreams and given us instead a continuous existence of terrible reality; and, in all this grim period, there has been no disillusionment greater than the world-wide disillusionment in the twin revolutionary doctrines of Marxism and North American continentalism.[37]

Creighton thought those "twin revolutionary doctrines" could be dismissed in a single sentence; Canada had a "distinct and separate political identity" and "stood consciously aloof" from the "commonplace revolutionary movements."[38] If this were true, it was not well supported by Creighton's arguments. His formulation of the "twin revolutionary doctrines'' was in most respects identical with the prevailing American view. The Cold War theologian Reinhold Neibuhr was expressing a similar two world model—the American forces of good resisting the communist forces of evil. Creighton had accepted the basic construct without question, but he sought a Canadian place within the model. What he actually opposed was not so much anti-communism or Americanism but the liberal view that Canada was helpless in the unfolding world struggle. It was a rejection of the conclusions of men like J.M.S. Careless who were pessimistic about Canada's role within the two worlds: ''it is by now a truism that we live in a two power world, where very few nations can hope to count as entities in the bleak pattern of world power.''[39]

Marxism, as well as Americanism, has had a larger role than Creighton could envisage. If Creighton were correct at last—no longer gullible or deceived—how is it that the disillusionment appears not to have been so world-wide after all? At the very least, the Cubans, the Khmer Rouge, the Vietnamese and others failed to get the message. And a New Left, some of it frighteningly Canadian, emerged in spite of Creighton's news that the ''extraordinarily bad fit'' of revolutionary ideology was exposed in the 1950s.[40]

As should be clear by these examples, Creighton, like the liberals he excoriated, had his politics and he let those politics influence him in his historical work. His perspective was essentially Cold Warriorite, is spite of his distancing himself and Canada from certain aspects of that struggle. The politics and ideologies he opposed were ''alien''; the values he cherished were essential Canadian truths.

The liberals were fundamentally in agreement with the conservatives as to the central features of Cold War society they differed in their ''pragmatism'' which meant greater limitations of Canadian autonomy and an acceptance of

American leadership in the struggle for the Free World. A.R.M. Lower articulated the position well in a 1962 speech "Armaments and Disarmaments." "Everybody shouts 'about communism'," Lower declared. "Some shout, rather less loudly, 'better dead than red'. I am among those who so shout."[41] Nationalism had clearly defined limits in the face of historic duty. Although Lower saw the development of the Canadian nation as an important historic theme, his "grip on realism" convinced him of the limited value of modern national politics. When the U.S. attempt to place nuclear weapons on Canadian soil was a central political issue, Lower defended the liberal-continentalists who supported American ambitions.

> The clash between the two lines of thought comes out well in the attitude of the ban-the-bombers of today. Very fine, well meaning people, no doubt they are, but have they any grip on realism? . . . I think that along with the nations outside the circle of the great powers, we ought to make, say, one more attempt to get the two big powers to moderate their atomic transports and then, if that fails, take up our position without qualification alongside the rest of the west. That means receiving on our own soil the atomic means of reprisal, to wit, completing the Bomarck installations.[42]

It was the same "two lines of thought" and "western world" as had been presented by Creighton, as well as Underhill and Careless. It was the same attack upon the rationality of those who disagreed; Lower's opponents had no grip on realism, Creighton's were the victims of superior propaganda. The establishment historians adopted an anti-radical stance which influenced their historical perspective. Yet the traditional view of the profession maintains that Left scholars are distinctive for politicizing their scholarship. Political expression in support of some model of the Cold

War was an expression of civic duty. But Left politics were circumscribed by the responsible limits of civil liberties, by the understanding that academic freedom was a term of art designed to promote a peculiar image of university autonomy, without granting licence to express controversial political perspectives.

That establishment historians in the United States were politicized is a central theme of the Lemisch paper; that the limits on political expression were carefully drawn is also documented. In Canada, somewhat similar evidence exists demonstrating a narrow but gradually expanding circumference of permissible expression. In 1959 Underhill declared: "in Canada it is still slightly improper for professors to become too interested in current politics."[43] In view of the many Cold War speeches which were not criticized, it seems necessary to amend this statement with more detail. Some academics have been criticized and penalized for their politics while others have not. Underhill himself put it more clearly, expressing a central theme of Lemisch's essay in Canadian terms in a March 1936 *Canadian Forum* article entitled "On Professors and Politics:"

> Why then the outraged indignation of so many respectable people at the present activity of a few professors in politics? Can it be that the real offense just now consists in the fact that the professors concerned have mostly taken the radical side? There have been several recent incidents affecting the teaching profession in Canada which make one wonder whether this may not be the real motive behind the solicitude for keeping our institutions of learning out of current controversy. We have the curious coincidence that when Professor Norman Rogers of Queen's goes into politics as a member of one of the respectable parties no question seems to arise as to the propriety of his actions, but when Professor W.H. Alexander of Alberta tries to run as a Labour candidate

his intrusion into politics is immediately discovered to be dangerous to his university. And a school principal in Regina, Mr. Coldwell, is forbidden by his board to engage in political activity, while another school principal in Calgary, Mr. Aberhart, launches a new party without his right to engage in politics ever being questioned. Did the different rulings of the two schoolboards have anything to do with the fact that Mr. Coldwell was a genuine radical and Mr. Aberhart was only a sham one, who incidentally, was also assisting powerfully in destroying the farmers' government in the province?[44]

One amazing aspect of the narrowness of legitimate academic debate is the extent to which liberals and conservatives have viewed themselves as different, while sharing an ideological stance hostile to any genuinely radical alternative. It was in the middle and late 1940s when Donald Creighton "began to realize just how radically the Liberal interpretation of Canadian history differed from [his] own."[45] At approximately the same point in time, A.R.M. Lower made a similar discovery while adopting the liberal perspective.[46] Yet, if we compare their views toward Marxism or radicalism, it is difficult to discover the substance of their differences. There are perhaps some stylistic variants in the hostility, but liberals and conservatives have reached a consensus beyond which dissent becomes intolerable.

Lower, who "was called of God to be an historian," took pride in his forthright stand in defence of free speech and civil liberties.[47] "My thoughts and pen were occupied with civil liberties," he wrote in his autobiography, yet his acts fit within the framework of liberal anti-communist ideology:

The Communists in Winnipeg testified to the significance of our Civil Liberties Association by their determined efforts to join it. We saw that, if we took them in, we would all be suspect and our cause made almost hopeless. Consequently, telephone calls were ignored and offers of aid were not

> accepted. . . . The stand I took as chairman was that we would cooperate with any group that did not have ulterior motives.[48]

What were the ulterior motives of the Communists? Across Canada, with World War II raging, an estimated one hundred and fifty members of the Party were herded into internment camps without trials; their politics were a threat to the security of the empire.[49] General civil libertarian principles did not protect communists when their views did not coincide with those of the government.

Academic freedom has not been a greater guarantee of the right to express oneself freely. In the 1890s MacKenzie King and other students at the University of Toronto went on strike to protest the University administration's cancellation of lectures by socialist Phillips Thompson and labour leader Alfred Jury.[50] The strike was opposed by Arthur Meighen who became a prominent figure in the Conservative party; King, the liberal politician, repudiated his student constituency and the first strike at the University of Toronto ultimately failed.

The situation was somewhat similar in the attempted firing of Frank Underhill from the University of Toronto History Department in the early 1940s. Underhill was still at that time a Fabian socialist and had been active in the formation of Canada's social democratic Cooperative Commonwealth Federation (subsequently the New Democratic Party). He had often been censured for controversial remarks and had entered into a gentleman's agreement with President Cody of the University of Toronto that he would not further speak out of turn. In the summer of 1940, however, Underhill again became a subject of controversy by committing the most cardinal of sins; he attacked the constitutional monarchy and the British connection. At a meeting of the Canadian

Institute of Economics and Politics at Lake Couchiching, Ontario, he was reported to have uttered a remark to the effect that the British flag should be made of wool that it might shrink with the rest of the empire.[51] His comments touched off an outraged indignation in important circles.

Senator Arthur Meighen wrote to the Minister of Justice deploring Underhill's conduct and asking that "an example be made of this man." Underhill's remarks were "disloyal"; "he and his ilk" should "be given to understand" that "they must behave."[52] A substantial portion of the press appealed to the Board of Governors to have Underhill dismissed. Premier Hepburn and other leaders of the Provincial Government were in agreement, but the Board failed to act upon the resolution.[53]

The Underhill controversy flared up a second time in January of 1941 after President Cody, in the 1890s tradition, cancelled another lecture by a labour leader. Sponsored by the C.C.F. Club, the lecture was entitled "Hepburn Must Go" and was labeled "indiscreet" by the University administration.[54] Underhill disagreed, and his continued controversial visibility rekindled the attempt to have him dismissed. Students, including C.C.F. Club President Kenneth McNaught, organized in support of the right to free speech, against the political attack and the closing of the University to a somewhat leftward point of view. Creighton was the only historian in the U. of T. Department who did not lend his name in support of Underhill's continued appointment.[55]

Underhill, essentially a liberal historian, kept his position, but it was not a significant victory for free speech or academic freedom.[56] Consensus in repression is the central lesson to be learned from what transpired. Among Underhill's unacknowledged supporters were members of the Young Communist League. When they in turn were

attacked for their politics, there was universal agreement
that the limits of free expression did not extend to Communists. The student newspaper, *The Varsity,* asked all
those students receiving the Young Communist League
leaflets in support of Underhill to bring them, with the
envelopes, to the paper offices in Hart House and University
College. The editors promised to collect the subversive
material and turn it over to the R.C.M.P.[57] The Secretary-
Treasurer of the Students' Administrative Council told a
Globe and Mail reporter: "They are getting very bold when
they will defy both the city police and the R.C.M.P."[58]

Conservatives, like Meighen or Creighton, have never
suffered from attempting to speak out in support of their
politics; they have seldom been confronted for attempting to
deny that right to others, Liberals and sometime social
democrats, King, Underhill, McNaught, *et al.*, moved part
way toward opening the range of dialogue within the university and that is perhaps significant. But the dialogue has
never been open and in each case there were some — Phillips
Thompson and the Young Communist leafleters — who were
excluded from participation altogether: they looked to a
more radical perspective and fared less well at the academy.

In part this may be explained by the very structures of the
University. In 1958, when Claude Bissell was invested as
President of the University of Toronto, Donald Creighton
was there to lend a hand. As chairman of the Department of
History, Creighton spoke on behalf of the faculty in welcom
ing Bissell to his new appointment.

> We are all here: heads of Universities and Colleges, deans
> and directors, chairmen of departments, senior professors
> and administrators, members of the Senate. These, sir, are
> your chief barons, the peers of the realm. For do not be
> deceived by the modern republican connotations of the word
> "president." The University of Toronto, like all the best

> governments in the world, is fundamentally a constitutional
> monarchy. Constitutional monarchies and universities are
> both creations of the medieval world; and what, in modern
> times, could be more emphatically medieval than the compli-
> cated relationships and hierarchies of this nineteenth century
> university?[59]

It was a nineteenth century university governed by medieval
principles; the same principles that Creighton had sought to
impose upon the Cold War and the general fabric of
Canadian society. The students and junior faculty were,
deliberately or inadvertently, absent from the ranks of
Creighton's "Peers of the Realm." By the end of the next
decade, they would be very much present and the inroads of
student power would soon make it unlikely that they would
ever be forgotten again. Like the also forgotten "lower
orders" of Creighton's cherished medieval past, the students were in revolt.

Within the universities and within the Canadian historical
profession an attitude hostile to radicalism has flourished.
We must incorporate an awareness of that fact into our
historical and social analysis. At the same time, we must be
careful in the way we interpret the evidence of anti-radical
bias. It may still be argued that things in Canada were
different from the events that Lemisch describes in the
United States. But there *is* a history of anti-radicalism within
Canadian universities and among Canadian historians. If
repression has in fact acted differently in Canada, it will only
be demonstrated by careful study of what has occurred. We
have a full length study of the American historical profession, but we have barely anticipated a similar attempt to
study Canada. To assert that Canada is the same or different,
it is necessary to do so comparatively on the basis of
research and the compilation of data. It is not necessary to
assert that there is a one to one relationship between events

in the two countries; it is not possible to ignore the important similarities.

IV.

The Lemisch essay on the U.S. historical profession presents a remarkable combination of history and current events. An anti-radical history manifested itself in the contemporary world through historians active in the processes of repression. The organization of the profession into a self-policing group and the archaic and hierarchical structures extant within the universities played a significant part in the closing of the university community to the radical voice.

Lemisch demonstrated that the American historians put their politics into the past in the characterization of what was important, of what took place as history. But he also exposed the workings of those same politics in the present, demonstrating many of the divergent forms which repression could take. Some radicals were fired or expelled, but as Lemisch documents, anti-radicalism often took more subtle forms. The extraordinary and well publicized case was not a particularly good measure of the extent of repression by hostile active conservatives and liberals. The graduate student ritual, the whole process by which one achieves status and recognition within the profession, has been designed to eliminate the ''politically unsuitable'' before they were ''admitted'' as practicing professional historians.

Once the historian was admitted or established within the profession, repression did not go away. In the early 1970s, as staid a body as the American Historical Association expressed concern for the rights of historians. A committee of inquiry was established to investigate violations of academic freedom and the dangers posed to the profession by such violations. The committee reported in late 1974 confirming the presence of widespread political fear among members of the historical profession:

> There is cause for concern about the state of academic freedom within the profession. Despite the fact that there can be no sure knowledge of the absolute level of infringement on the rights of historians nor any firm basis for knowing whether the trend is up or down, there are many allegations of unfair treatment and there is ample evidence that a significant proportion of the profession perceives injustices being done.
>
> The sources of these threats to academic freedom are multifold. Though historians view administrations and Boards of Governors with more suspicion in this regard than they view faculty groups, history departments themselves are not immune from criticism.[60]

It might be added that a survey dominated by the views of established faculty members is somewhat misleading in establishing the sources of threats to academic freedom. While the report noted inadequacies in insuring fairness in initial appointments, academic freedom is still largely construed in terms of advanced scholars with established credentials. In practice, rights are determined by the place occupied in the system. Departments may be the single most repressive element in controlling the thoughts and lives of students; deans and senior administrators could still be the source of pressures brought to bear on senior members of the faculty.

Additionally, status within the university and higher education network is not the entire determinant. Privileged access—and lack of access—to source materials can be crucial factors in establishing who can write what kind of history. To a large degree, a handful of editors associated with a small number of scholarly journals retain the capacity to decide which historical work will be disseminated to the broader historical profession.

The description in this introduction of the way Lemisch's manuscript was received is but one example of a more general reaction, a more general process of exclusion. Not every form of repression ends in an overt fight at the barricades. The resignation of Marlene Dixon from the Sociology Department at McGill University in Montreal in 1975 is an important case of a phenomenon much more widespread. When she came up for re-appointment, she chose not to go through the process. Had she done so, she might very well have secured her position on the basis of her scholarship, in spite of her left politics. Nonetheless, she chose not to fight and she made it clear that it was an atmosphere of perceived repression at McGill that was responsible for her decision. To be victorious, within the context of a hostile environment, is to be a partial victim —unable to work effectively, unable to lead a fully meaningful life.[61]

Anti-radicalism within the universities did not end in 1969 when Lemisch completed his manuscript. The subversion of academic radicalism has continued. There is an immense amount of data with which to update a critique of the kind made by Lemisch.[62] The passing of the era of the New Left creates an illusion of campus tranquility which belies the reality. Repression, which was exposed in moments of movement strength—such as the Lemisch presentation at the American Historical Association Convention—continues unabated and now largely unmitigated by a radical student presence.

Tolerance that greeted early movement activism disappeared as liberals learned that they could not channel radical grievances into a limited demand for reforms that corresponded with their own liberal objectives. The New Left was

viewed benignly while it was a distant force, but hysteria and
open repression emerged when the New Left continued as a
significant movement in opposition to liberal and conservative politics. The most brutal repression has occurred in the
years after Lemisch wrote his essay. Nowhere is the change
in attitude more clearly portrayed than in the eidtorial pages
of the *Journal of Canadian Studies*.

In 1968 the *Journal* editors looked upon the student
movement calmly, expecting more activism, but still aware
that there were understandable causes and legitimate grievances underlying the world-wide student actions:

> Last autumn's student demonstrations at Sir George Wil-
> liams and McGill Universties seem small stuff beside the
> anarchic displays of power at Columbia, in the West German
> Easter riots, and at the University of Paris. These infectious
> manifestations, while each rooted in local circumstances,
> imply important things in common about modern univer-
> sities, centralized political authority, and the goals of indus-
> trial society. The startling impact of "student power" in
> 1968, and the momentum created in dozens of places in the
> western world, make virutally certain that militant student
> action will continue rather than fade away. Behind events,
> too, there are structural changes that will sustain this action.

Three years later the editors voiced a much greater degree of
alarm —though the events they pointed to were much less
dramatic. The attitude of students was absolutely dangerous
and the fight was on for the preservation of civilization:

> An interested observer may be permitted to comment that
> the real threat to civilized political life may not come from
> either an unchecked liberalism or (as the liberals may have it)
> from a reactionary and irrational conservatism but from
> something which stands against both. It is necessary to con-
> sider whether liberalism and conservatism are in some sense
> allies in a common stronghold which is now under

siege.

. . .

We should not fool ourselves: the present attack upon the political process is not just an attack upon our particular political institutions or upon the "old parties" (for which read all parties). It is an attack upon civilizaiton itself.

. . .

The rejection of rational thought . . . on the part of intellectuals is reflected, amplified, and taken by their students to its inevitable conclusion. . . . To give only one minor example: a recent front-page editorial on university government in the Carleton student paper sneered at the faculty ("being members of the intellectual elite") for believing that "all things can be solved through reason rather than power struggles".

This is the real crisis of civilization. . . . It is also the special problem of those of us who are involved in the work of the universities, whose primary concerns are the activities of our own minds and the activity of those minds who it is our task to educate.[64]

The editorial indicates that repression is alive and well —with old themes from the fifties and sixties carried on into the seventies. At the same time it demonstrates the manner in which repression can escalate and change its form. The very existence of hostile political remarks in such a journal raises issues. The political orientation which led to the establishment of the American Studies movement in the United States is described by Lemisch. Canadian Studies is an analogue; similar concerns led to its development. The *Journal of Canadian Studies,* and by implication the conservative editorial politics expressed therein, are a product of the Canadian Studies Programme at Trent University in Peterborough, Ont. a programme financially backed by the Ford Motor Company of Canada.[65] Canada's largest corporation, like other groups in society, has an interest in nationalism and in the political directions of the nationalist movements. In a more general sense, universities continue to respond to the business and governmental interests that sustain their existence.

The American-Canadian analogue should not surprise us. What has happened in the United States also happens in Canada for understandable reasons. The interaction between the two societies is intense; as long ago as 1928 Frank Underhill was urging Canadian historians to ''set ourselves to study what American historians are doing in the rewriting of American history.''[66] And to Creighton's lament, many historians did so. If that U.S. history was political, conservative, anti-radical, what effect did that have upon the Canadians who set forth to study it?

During the 1960s the Canadian university system grew extremely rapidly; whole departments were staffed with academics originating from the U.S. campuses described by Lemisch. A few were radicals in search of asylum. But many were conservative professors expatriating themselves in hopes of avoiding the political protest that surged across the United States; when they crossed the border they found many like-minded Canadians who shared their reactionary point of view. In addition, the structure and purposes of Canadian and American universities are similar. Where the structures foster authoritarianism, hierarchy, elitism, and conservatism, some form of protest and response can perhaps be anticipated regardless of the location. Much of the student movement of the 1960s was international, emerging in Europe, in Canada, and in the United States.

Moreover, Canadians have traditionally gone to U.S. graduate schools in great numbers. The attitudes encountered there have shaped the Canadian culture and university system in diverse subtle and unsubtle ways. In the wake of general and growing concern over the meaning of such influence, any in-depth study of the politics of the American academy is of immense interest.

Anti-radicalism remains difficult to document. It occurs in sylvan Burnaby, B.C. as well as New Haven, at junior colleges as well as major universities. And the combined working of repression and tolerance continue as the New Left, to use Lemisch's own description, recedes back into the quotation marks from which it came. When radicals are not strong, they can be ignored in general or destroyed when they act on their principles. A senior and conservative professor at the State University of New York at Buffalo recently pronounced that the "New Left was as dead as Banquo's ghost." But when he asserted that in his department "of approximately thirty-five men, there is no one you could say was of the New Left persuasion," he neglected to add that Gabriel Kolko and others had left Buffalo in justified anticipation of the repression of a new university administration; that Lemisch was across cmpus but not in the history department; that a few women, some active in New Left politics, were subsumed under the description "approximately thirty-five men."[67]

On that same campus, in May of 1975, ten students were arrested and many injured, when university administrators vetoed student government plans for support of the Attica Brothers, victims in a series of current political trials stemming from the prison uprising of September 1971.[68] Suspensions followed the "Due Process" guidelines which had emerged under liberal impetus as universities sought to define the fashion in which they would deal with dissent. The arrests also demonstrate the developments arising from the 1960s whereby police—and sometimes armies—have become a legitimate presence on campuses. Long gone are the days of the self-governing and self-policing university. The alliance between administrators and outside firepower has become entrenched, and through usage is now largely unquestioned.

This writer is not an expert on the subject of repression in the years since 1969. In referring to specific cases, it is not always possible to discern the patterns or to establish the identity of victims on a broad scale. What follows is admittedly impressionistic and incomplete. To present anything like an accurate or complete picture would require a tremendous amount of research. But most of us know of specific cases on campuses where we live or work, on campuses with which we are familiar. Those cases exist in sufficient quantity, and have been sufficiently documented in the press, so as to support the thesis that intense repression is present in a campus atmosphere marked by insecurity, economic uncertainty, and the scramble for grades or tenure.

One might consider the role of senior administrators and government officials in the decisions not to hire Professor John Seeley at the University University of Toronto and the Ontario Institute for Studies in Education; one might be concerned by the active role of such historians as W.H. Nelson, J.B. Conacher, Desmond Morton, Kenneth McNaught, and Michael Bliss in the emotional condemnation which led to subsequent suspension of graduate students Bill Schabas and Tony Leah for their acts in opposition to the on-campus presence of Edward Banfield at the University of Toronto. Some of those historians labeled the student demonstrators "thugs" and wrote of the importance of preserving academic freedom. Yet, when Seeley, whom they considered to be of the Left, was denied due process in the consideration of his appointment they remained strangely silent and their views on academic freedom could not be heard.[70]

Equally disturbing is the political firing of Jeffrey Forest and Hugh Miller at Renison College in Waterloo, Ontario;[71]

and the continued struggle for re-instatement of Mordecai Briemberg and others purged from the Political Science-Socology-Anthropology Department at Simon Fraser University in Burnaby, B.C.[72] There is a struggle taking place between radical and establishment economists on many campuses; in many instances—including San Jose State University in California, Lehman College in New York City, and the University of Massachusetts in Boston—that struggle is resulting in political dismissals and the loss of jobs.[73] In Arizona, FBI agents sent an anonymous derogatory letter to a college committee reviewing a radical philosopher's teaching contract.[74]

Such examples could be continued for an extensive number of pages. Still, some may see cause for optimism in several recent developments. The Committee for the Rights of Historians within the American Historical Association has come up with an orderly set of guidelines in a move towards protecting the job rights of historians. On the one hand, the committee and its work represents a step forward in the struggle for due process; on the other hand, there are features of the report that are inadequate—especially in establishing protection for divergent life styles and in the implementation of enforcement procedures. With the exception of discussion, enforcement is left in the hands of the American Association of University Professors as it was in the past.[75] Similarly, much has been made of Affirmative Action Programs and the active recruitment of Blacks, women and other minorities on U.S. campuses. It may represent some progress, but there is ample evidence that much alleged compliance is a mere sham; that many universities are unwilling or unable to bring about effective change in a significant fashion.[76] Like protective factory legislation for women in the late nineteenth century, liberal efforts to redress the shameful practices of discrimination and exploitation may lead to other abuses causing yet other kinds of harm.

On the broad view, it is not possible to adequately discuss the subject of repression in the 1970s in a short essay. Its theoretical underpinnings and practical effects are too complex to emerge without detailed study. Nonetheless, repression has its effect, in part governing the way historians and other academics are hired and fired, in determining the kind of work they can do and the kind of reception it will receive. It has a hand in the kind of programmes that are established and funded, and in the curtailment of other kinds of inquiry. Repressive forces help to dictate which interests are served on campuses and they emerge in alliances with cops and guns in the supression and coercion of "subversive elements". At the same time, the workings of repression can be more subtle, effecting a kind of tolerance for dissent that exists within the rules while simultaneously placing intolerable burdens on those who it appears to tolerate. As one reads the Lemisch essay with its details of past horrors, it is important to keep in mind the ways in which the struggle continues. All is not history; repression is a continuing part of our immediate daily lives.

V.

It remains perhaps curious that this manuscript is being published in Canada, although its content deals exclusively with U.S. historians and events centered on U.S. campuses. The reasoning is easily explained. The interlocking nature of higher education—especially as between the two countries—has been discussed and is easily documented. Events centered in the United States are important in the repercussions they have in Canada and elsewhere.

Secondly, Lemisch's study is important as a statement of the possibilities, going far beyond the actual subject matter he undertakes. As part of an expanding literature which critically examines the professionalization of knowledge and the role of the University in curbing radicalism within the academic disciplines, it demonstrates what can be done methodologically.[77] The reader can translate from this data to other subject areas—political economy or perhaps English literature—until a gradually developing critique encompasses the entirety of higher education. Lemisch presents a general invitation to consider the masked content, the politics, of scholarship. We are convinced that his invitation can only be profitably accepted.

Thirdly, what Lemisch has written about the U.S. historical profession is of particular importance to an analysis of Canadian history. As this introduction has gone some way to suggest, the evidence is available to compile a similar study. Parallel themes seem to emerge. It is not yet possible to assert with confidence that the situation is the same or different. But it is impossible to dismiss the questions without the careful compilation of data.

The central thrust of Lemisch's paper is the questioning of history as it has thus far been written. The sharp exposure of the myths that uphold the U.S. historical profession points to the general vulnerability of establishment history written in defence of establishment politics. It suggests the value of such a critique and encourages the research which will uncover the past in Canada—both within and without the academy.

Finally, Canadian and American academics—like employers, Premiers, and Governors—have often linked their fortunes. To their great lament, radicals have sometimes responded with a fraternalism of their own. In 1841, Major General M'leod of the Patriot Army described the events of the late uprising in Upper Canada. He advised that "the friends of freedom" not despair, and directed his work to a distinct audience:

> The work is designed for the information of those numerous generous hearted citizens of the United States, who so nobly and manfully avowed their sympathy for the oppressed Canadians. . . .

By publishing Lemisch's paper in Canada, we may continue that respect among "the friends of freedom". For as M'leod asserted in 1841: "The contest is only suspended, not given up. The people are getting prepared, they will succeed."[78]

NOTES

1. Ronald Radosh, "Annual Set-to: The Bare-Knuckled Historians," *The Nation*, February 2, 1970, reprinted in Blanche W. Cook, Alice K. Harris, Ronald Radosh, eds., *Past Imperfect: Alternative Essays in American History* (New York: Alfred Knopf, 1973) II, pp. 339-41.
2. *New York Times*, January 15, 1970, p. 46.
3. Correspondence, R.K. Webb to Jesse Lemisch, March 27, 1970.
4. *Ibid*.
5. Correspondence, Martin Ridge to Jesse Lemisch, July 17, 1970.
6. Telephone conversation between Martin Ridge and Jesse Lemisch, July 20, 1970.
7. Garry Wills, "From Here to There," *The Spectrum*, November 6, 1974, p. 9.
8. Unidentified reader's comments accompanying Ridge's letter to Lemisch. The customary academic procedure of not identifying readers may itself be questioned. Anonymity may be used as a kind of shield from responsibility for the kind of remarks cited above.
9. Correspondence, John Higham to Jesse Lemisch, November 26, 1969. See also: Higham, "Beyond Consensus: The Historian as Moral Critic," *American Historical Review*, LXVII (1962), pp. 609-25.
10. *Newsweek*, December 23, 1974, pp. 18-19; for the menu see: *Time*, December 23, 1974, p. 10 (American edition).
11. For a discussion of this point, see: Lemisch *infra*, footnotes 71 and 126.
12. E.P. Thompson, "An Open Letter to Leszek Kolakowski," in Ralph Miliband and John Saville, eds., *The Socialist Register, 1973* (London: The Merlin Press, 1974), p. 89. Thompson addressed his comments within the Left and assumes good faith. The liberal anti-communists who are guilty in Lemisch's data are in fact aware of the significance of their acts. While presenting themselves as upholders of free debate, they know that the doctrine they espouse functions to close that debate.
13. [Joseph Featherstone] "Scholars and Society," *The New Republic*, January 17, 1970, pp. 7-8.
14. See: Lemisch, "History, Complete With Historian." For complete citation, see: "About the Author."
15. For a general discussion, see: Frank Cunningham, *Objectivity In Social Science* (Toronto: University of Toronto Press, 1973).
16. See also: Naomi Weisstein, Virginia Blaisdell, and Jesse Lemisch,

The Godfathers: Marxians, Freudians, and the Scientific and Political Protection Societies.

17. For full citations, see: "About the Author."

18. Robin Winks, "Canada," in Robin Winks, ed. *The Historiography of the British Empire-Commonwealth* (Durham, N.C.: Duke University Press, 1966), pp. 80, 125.

19. A.R.M. Lower, *Canadians in the Making, a Social History of Canada* (Don Mills, Ontario: Longmans Canada, Ltd., 1958), p. 419.

20. D.G. Creighton, "Presidential Address," Canadian Historical Association, *Annual Report* (Toronto, 1957), p. 7. The question is not whether there is truth in the description that radicalism is weak. These historians not only underestimate its strength, but they also assert that such a state of weakness is normal and necessary.

21. Hilda Neatby, "On the Dangers of History," *La Nouvelle Revue Canadienne* I (July, 1951), p. 27.

22. Gad Horowitz, *Canadian Labour in Politics* (Toronto: University of Toronto Press, 1968), p. 84.

23. Gad Horowitz, "On The Fear of Nationalism," *Canadian Dimension*, IV (May-June, 1967), pp. 8-9.

24. John Bartlet Brebner, "Canadian and North American History," Canadian Historical Association, *Annual Report* (Ottawa, 1931), p. 42.

25. H.N. Fieldhouse, "Liberalism in Crisis," Canadian Historical Association, *Annual Report* (Toronto, 1940), p. 106.

26. Frank H. Underhill, *In Search of Canadian Liberalism* (Toronto: Macmillan Company of Canada Limited, 1960), p. 12ff.

27. Stanley Bréhaut Ryerson, *The Founding of Canada: Beginnings to 1815,* (Toronto: Progress Books, 1960); *Unequal Union: Confederation and The Roots of Conflict in the Canadas 1815-1873* (New York: International Publishers, 1968); for Ryerson's criticism of numerous Anglo-Canadian historians, including G.P. de T. Glazebrook, Edgar McInnis, J.M.S. Careless, and K. McNaught, see: "'Race,' 'Nationality,' and the Anglo-Canadian Historians," *Canadian Jewish Outlook*, XI, no. 6 (July, 1973), pp. 3-4, 12.

28. Gustave Lanctot, "Review: *The Founding of Canada*, by Stanley Ryerson," *Canadian Historical Review*, XLII (1961), p. 147.

29. Frank H. Underhill, *op. cit.*, 255.

30. Donald Grant Creighton, "Canada and the Cold War," in *Towards the Discovery of Canada, Selected Essays* (Toronto: Macmillan of Canada, 1972), p. 245.

31. D.G. Creighton, "Presidential Address," 10.

32. *Ibid.*, 4.

38

33. *Ibid.*, 5.
34. *Ibid.*, 4; but compare Creighton's criticism of this development with the favourable account by Claude Bissell: "... in Ottawa no great separation between town and gown exists ... our community extends far beyond our academic walls." Claude T. Bissell, Preface to the Alan B. Plaunt Memorial lectures: *Canada and its Giant Neighbour*, by Jacob Viner presented and published at Carleton University, Ottawa, January 30-February 1, 1958.
35. D.G. Creighton, "Presidential Address," 4.
36. *Ibid.*, 6.
37. *Ibid.*, 11.
38. *Ibid.*
39. J.M.S. Careless, "Canadian Nationalism—Immature or Obsolete?", Canadian Historical Association, *Annual Report* (Toronto, 1954), p. 13.
40. *Ibid.*, 10.
41. A.R.M. Lower, "Armaments and Disarmaments," Fourth Annual Seminar On Canadian-American Relations (Assumption University), *Proceedings* (Windsor, Ontario: 1962), p. 113.
42. *Ibid.*, 129.
43. Frank H. Underhill, *op. cit.*, 269.
44. Frank H. Underhill, "On Professors and Politics," *Canadian Forum*, March 1936, reprinted in *Forum: Canadian Life and Letters 1920-1970*, J.L. Granatstein and Peter Stevens, eds. (Toronto: University of Toronto Press, 1972), p. 141.
45. Donald Grant Creighton, "Presidential Address," 5.
46. For Lower's account of his adoption of liberal politics, see: A.R.M. Lower, *My First Seventy Five Years* (Toronto: Macmillan of Canada, 1967), pp. 138-39; for his view of historians and politics generally see: *The Craft of History*, Eleanor Cook, ed., with an introduction by Ramsay Cook, (Toronto: CBC Publications, 1973), pp. 8, 38.
47. Lower himself points out the call from God in a television interview with Ramsay Cook, *Ibid.*, 2.
48. A.R.M. Lower, *My First Seventy-five Years*, 237.
49. See, for example: Leopold Infeld, "The Story of Samuel Levine," *Canadian Forum*, November 1941, pp. 245-47; during this period the *Forum* was carrying a regular feature "Civil Liberties." The column cites extensive repression under the Defence of Canada Regulations then in effect. After the Russians entered the war, a Communist-Liberal alliance emerged and the Regulations were eased with respect to enforcement against Communists.

50. *The Varsity*, March 14, 1941, p. 3ff; H.S. Ferns and B. Ostry, *The Age of Mackenzie King* (London: William Heinemann, Ltd., 1955), pp. 20-29.

51. Maxwell Cohen, "Couchiching," *Canadian Forum*, XX, No. 237, (October 1940), p. 200.

52. Roger Graham, *Arthur Meighan*, III, (Toronto: Clarke, Irwin & Co., 1965), p. 123.

53. Toronto, *Globe and Mail*, January 11, 1941, p. 4.

54. *The Varsity*, December 5, 1940, p. 1.

55. For an on campus view, see: *The Varsity*, January 9, 1941; January 13, 1941 (Editorial); January 28, 1941.

56. For the nature of the defence of Underhill, see: Carlton McNaught, "Democracies and Our Universities," *Canadian Forum*, XX No. 241, (February, 1941), p. 333. Underhill's repudiation of radicalism is contained in Frank Hawkins Underhill, *The Radical Tradition: A Second View of Canadian History;* the texts of two half-hour radio programs by Frank H. Underhill and Paul Fox, as originally presented on the CBC television network in the program "Explorations," June 8th and 15th, 1960 (Toronto: CBC Publications, 1961).

57. *The Varsity*, January 28, 1941, p. 1.

58. Toronto *Globe and Mail*, January 29, 1941, p. 4.

59. *The Installation of Claude Thomas Bissell, Eighth President*, "Welcome Home II," Welcoming Address by Donald G. Creighton, Chairman of the Department of History.

60. "The Rights of Historians: An AHA Report," *AHA Newsletter*, XII, No. 9 (December 1974), p. 9; for a report on implementation, see "Implementation of the Hackney Report," *AHA Newsletter*, XIII, No.4 (April 1975), p. 1. Copies of the Final Report of the Committee on the Rights of Historians are available from the American Historical Association.

61. See: Marlene Dixon, "Letter of Resignation," *Insurgent Sociologist*, V, No. 11 (Winter 1975), pp. 51-64.

62. Some of Lemisch's writings since 1969 can be seen as furthering his general critique. See: "Radical Plot in Boston (1770): A Study in the Use of Evidence," and parts of "The American Revolution Bicentennial and the Papers of Great White Men," and "The White Oaks, Jack Tar, and the Concept of the 'Inarticulate'"[with John K. Alexander]. For full citations, see "About the Author."

63. "Editorial," *Journal of Canadian Studies*, III, No. 2 (May 1968), p. 1.

64. Editorial: "The Dialectic of Mind: Some Thoughts on Reason and Civility," *Journal of Canadian Studies*, VI, No. 1 (February 1971),

pp. 1-2, 63-64.

65. Canadian Studies, Trent University, 1974-1975 brochure.

66. Frank Underhill, "Canadian and American History—and Historians," *Canadian Forum*, August 1928, reprinted in *Forum: Canadian Life and Letters*, pp. 58-60.

67. Remarks by Professor Selig Adler to his graduate "Research Seminar in American Historiography," State University of New York at Buffalo, July 1974.

68. *The Spectrum*, April 28, 1975, p. 1; May 2, 1975, p. 1.

69. Seeley's appointment to the Sociology Department at the University of Toronto was blocked by the highest levels of the administration including the Dean of the Faculty of Arts and Science, the Dean of theGraduate school, and Provost Donald Forster of the central administration of the University. The routine staffing decision of the department was rejected *before* the Departmental Chairman could recommend the appointment in the normal fashion. See: *The Varsity*, January 8, 1975 and prior issues, October through December 1974. At OISE the appointment was denied after intervention by high government officials. The following discolsure was made on the floor of the Ontario Legislature by Conservative Party Education Minister Tom Wells:

> Hon. Mr. Wells:
> . . . it comes to mind, six months or so ago, one or two prominent educators in this province phoned me and indicated that they thought it would be bad for OISE if John Seeley were appointed there. I did communicate this information to the director, because these were very respected educators of this province. I communicated that information to the director and indicated to him that I'd had these calls. So I don't want to leave you with the impression that somehow I had never known about this. These calls were made to me about six months ago, but since then I haven't heard anything more about it. . . . As I say, I do not know Prof. Seeley, but I guess he realizes that he is a controversial figure. . . .
>
> Mr. Foulds:
> I don't know if you understand the importance of what you have just said. What you have said is that you intervened. . . . It seems to be—if I may say so, and I say it with great respect—that you were manipulating.
>
> Hon. Mr. Wells:
> No.
>
> Mr. Foulds:
> Then you deliberately passed on hearsay evidence. That's not very good behaviour for a minister of the Crown.
>
> Hon. Mr. Wells:
> It is not hearsay evidence.

An Hon. Member:
Corporal Punishment.

Mr. B. Gilbertson:
Oh, come on.

Hansard, Ontario Legislature, November 7, 1974 pp. 5025-5026.

70. See: *The Varsity*, March 20, 1974; Desmond Morton, Letter: "Professor Deplores U. of T. Tolerance of Thugs," *Globe and Mail*, March 16, 1974; John W. Robson, W.H. Nelson, J.B. Conacher, J.S. Dupre, Allan Bloom, Letter: *Globe and Mail*, March 18, 1974; Michael Bliss: "Professor Protests Fracas by U. of T. Storm Troopers," *Toronto Star*, March 16, 1974; Kenneth McNaught, editorial: "James Shaver Woodsworth," *Canadian Forum*, September 1974, p. 2; The University of Toronto *Graduate*, October 1974, p. 9ff.

71. *The Chevron*, November 15, 1974; January 31, 1975.

72. See: Daniel Drache, "The Simon Fraser Blacklist," *This Magazine*, VIII, No. 4 (Nov.-Dec. 1974), pp. 10-11; Mordecai Briemberg, "A Taste of Better Things," *This Magazine is About Schools*, IV, No.1 (Winter 1970), pp. 32-55; Katheleen Gough, "The Struggle at Simon Fraser," *Monthly Review*, May 1970.

73. Soma Golden, "Radical Economists Under Fire," *New York Times*, February 2, 1975; Lawrence F. Lifscultz, "Could Karl Marx Teach Economics in America?" *Ramparts*, XII, No.9 (April 1974), p. 27ff.

74. Nocholas M. Horrock, "F.B.I. Data Tells of Harassment of Teacher," *New York Times*, January 29, 1975, p. 12; Harry Ring, "Secret FBI Memos Reveal 'Disruption' Conspiracy Against Socialist Professor," *The Militant*, February 14, 1975, p. 13, contains reproductions of the FBI documents.

75. See note 60.

76. Sheila K. Johnson, "It's Action, But Is It Affirmative?" *New York Times*, Magazine, Sunday May 11, 1975, p.18ff.

77. See, for example, the critique of establishment sociology in Herman and Julia Schwendinger, *The Sociologists of the Chair* (New York: Basic Books, 1974).

78. D. M'Leod, Major General, Patriot Army, Upper Canada. *A Brief Review of the SETTLEMENT OF UPPER CANADA by the U.E. LOYALISTS AND SCOTCH HIGHLANDERS, In 1783; And of the grievances which Compelled the Canadas to Have Recourse to Arms In Defence of Their RIGHTS AND LIBERTIES, in the years 1837 and 1838: together with a brief sketch of the CAMPAIGNS OF 1812, '13, '14: with an account of the Military Executions, Burnings,*

and Sackings of Towns and Villages by the British, in the Upper and Lower Provinces, during the COMMOTION OF 1837 and '38. (Cleveland: F.B. Penniman, 1841), p. 1.

I. Introduction:
The "Present-Mindedness" of the
New Left

In April of 1967, the Organization of American Historians
devoted a session of its annual meeting to "American
Historiography and the New Left." While several of the
accused New Left historians lurked about the—would you
believe?—Red Lacquer Room of Chicago's Palmer House,
and while one even sat on the dais, Professor Irwin Unger
discussed their work.[1]

"No discipline should be without a dialogue," said Unger:
it was healthy for profession, and "in any case the questions
the Left asks are . . . apt to be the interesting ones." But
what of the Left's *answers?* The New Left was, he said,
"negative," "bellicose," "acerbic," and their "conviction
of America's total depravity" led them to a history which
Unger often seemed to think so absurd that merely to
summarize it was to refute it.[2] Plunging into the New Left's
psyche, Unger wondered whether the "real purpose" of one
of them was "to dethrone the leading representatives of the
'establishment'." He saw others striking "an adolescent
blow for independence" in their attack on the New Deal: "in
rejecting it they are rejecting their fathers and their fathers'
faith."[3]

"Present-mindedness" was the central theme of Unger's
critique. In its view of America's earlier foreign relations,
the New Left was "obviously projecting onto history its
present cold war fears and frustrations." Their "harsh
judgment of nineteenth-century reform" was dictated, "in
the first place," not by the facts, but by "ideological
predispositions." In these and in other areas, the New Left

was using "scholarship as an opportunity for a political harangue," showing a contempt for what Unger called "pure history" ("history that has not enlisted in the good fight"), and instead was confusing "the truths of the past with the needs of the present and future."[4]

In their present-mindedness the New Left had revealed a "bad temper" and had "often failed to play the scholarly game by the most elementary rules of fair play," allowing "the tone and rhetoric of the picket line and the handbill to invade their professional work." There was, Unger felt, a kind of paranoia here, a "sense of persecution." And, since their fear that an "academic establishment" might use its "professional power to proscribe dissent and encourage conformity" was "largely anticipatory," it seemed, in Unger's word, "excessive."[5]

As it happens, the fears of American Left academics are not so much anticipatory as retrospective, based on a conservative reading of history which says that, unfortunately, the future may *not* turn out to be so different from the past. As we shall see, a very selective perception and memory on the part of non-Left historians has obscured the horror of the 'fifties—which were not so long ago. In its memory of the 'fifties, and the 'forties, and of the decades before, the New Left shows itself to be more respectful of the past than are its ahistorical critics.[6]

As for the 'sixties, by the time David Donald's polemical review of *Towards a New Past* appeared in the *American Historical Review,*[7] the evidence for his claim that New Left historians were at prestige universities was thirty-three per cent too optimistic.[8] Some time before Unger had spoken, Norman Pollack had left Yale. At the time, Staughton Lynd was following a similar path.[9] I had been dropped by the University of Chicago after my first term as assistant professor because, as the chairman of the history department explained, "Your convictions interfered with your scholarship."[10] During the summer after Unger spoke, Lynd was denied one job at Chicago State College—explicitly because of his "public activities"—and another at the University of Chicago, because he showed "bad judgment" in commenting on my own experience there. Meanwhile and subsequently, Lynd was rejected by a number of other institutions in the Chicago area, including one whose president explained that his reasons for vetoing an appointment were "ad hominem."

Lynd's experience has been the worst of those mentioned: in plain English, he is being blacklisted. But the employment picture for Left historians has not been all bad, and many have good jobs. On the other hand, even the most successful among them have found their opportunities narrowed by their politics.[11] Some of those with tenure have been frozen out by their departments in diverse subtle ways, and sometimes not so subtly.

But in repression, as in other matters, the view from the top down is inaccurate: we do not measure what is happening in a society so much through the experience of those whose names we *have* heard as through the experience of those whose names we have *not* heard. For many of these, especially younger radicals in graduate school and dependents within an atrocious hierarchy of caprice and injustice, for them political discrimination has been blatant. Expulsions, loss of fellowships, and poison pen letters of non-recommendation are common. All in all, although the radical voice on campus is far from silent, there is abundant evidence of attempts to suppress it. The radical teacher knows that someone in his class is taking notes for the FBI, the House Un-American Activities Committee, or the local red squad,[12] and he knows that, for all the talk of violence on campus, the most violent things which have happened on

American campuses have been the killing of Blacks at Orangeburg[13] and the nearly successful attempt to murder and to mutilate Left sociology professor Richard Flacks in his University of Chicago office.[14] To dismiss so lightly as did Unger the reality of repression is to lend support to it.*

So this is more than a tempest in a Palmer House. The sociology and politics of the academic world—which views are rewarded, which penalized, and, and, more simply, who is fired and who is hired—directly affect our view of America's past and thus of its present and future. Unger spoke of those historians who seemed to him to be unwilling to play by the rules of the game. What of those who *make* and *enforce* the rules? Here Unger found little to criticize. It was true, he acknowledged, that some of the New Left's elders had been influenced by "a conservative political bias" and exhibited a "self-congratulatory" quality; but "more common among them" was "a political neutrality which, however inadequate for citizenship, is certainly useful for scholarship."[15]

II. Repression after World War II

It is the purpose of this paper to examine the contention that American historiography since World War II has been politically neutral.[16] A full account would have to begin with the central fact of American politics in those years: the Cold

* In 1969, when Lemisch was writing, the most violent acts on campus were yet to come. His examples now seem temperate in the wake of the Kent State and Jackson State Massacres in the Spring of 1970. Though we are often told these days that the campuses have "returned to the 'fifties" in their complaisance, it is not certain that the most violent occurrences are behind us. And as the Lemisch account of the 'fifties makes clear—if it were true that students have returned to a former time, those times were grim ones. —editor's note

War. We cannot undertake a re-examination of foreign policy here. But we can note that a new revisionism[17] is suggesting that the non-Left which uses the passive-sounding term, "containment," while recoiling at "imperialism," may be less precise and further from cool analysis than are the wild activists whose abuse of the language they abhor; that, while Joe Stalin was hardly the avuncular old fellow portrayed by *Life* magazine during World War II, he may have been weak and acquiescent in 1945, and less aggressive than Harry Truman; that a proper attention to historical continuities will show that the Soviet Union of the 'sixties, known to the international New Left as hardly the friend, and—together with its subordinate Communist Parties—often the enemy of revolution, is, in that sense, little different from the nationalist Soviet Union of the 'forties; and that the same attention to continuity will show that such barbarities as Vietnam, far from being aberrations, are consistent with a central trend in American foreign policy. And this new revisionism, resting partly on the reading of documents unavailable at the time but also on information and an analysis which was readily available to any critical mind at the time, is suggesting that it was quite possible to see through both sides of the Cold War as it was happening.

External aggressiveness, internal repression:[18] those were the years of what has come to be called McCarthyism. But McCarthy did not invent McCarthyism: consider the 1946 Wisconsin senatorial campaign, in which Joe hopped on the anti-Communist bandwagon only after Norman Thomas* had suggested (at the forty-sixth annual picnic of the Wisconsin Socialist Party) that McCarthy's opponent was a "fellow-traveler."[19] Writing in 1950, Carey McWilliams

* Long-time leader of the U.S. Socialist Party and its perennial presidential candidate. —editor's note

described McCarthyism as the "direct outgrowth" of Harry Truman's 1947 loyalty program. In words which go far to suggest how repression starts in this country—from above, not below—McWilliams went on to say that "it was a foregone conclusion" that once a loyalty test had been set up, someone else would come along to challenge the adequacy of the test.[20]

The almost total failure of non-Left historians critically to examine liberal anti-communism is one aspect of the present-mindedness of these historians. A full exploration of this topic is beyond the scope of this paper. Suffice it to say that when the domestic history of the Cold War is written, it will take a new look at people like Thomas and Truman, and at the anti-communist clauses of such organizations as the American Civil Liberties Union and the Committee for a Sane Nuclear Policy.[21] It will note that liberals were no less anti-communist than McCarthy: what they opposed was the anti-communism which competed with and disrupted what they saw as the necessary anti-communism of government agencies.[22] And the logic of liberals led them to see the liberal's proper role as one of cooperation. Leslie Fiedler urged what he described as "a troubled and difficult course what seems to me the truly liberal one"—speak against McCarthy while naming names ("as if to 'rat' were the worst of crimes").[23] Arthur Schlesinger, Jr.'s patience grew short with those who felt that it was "somehow below the belt even to report on Communist Party activities or to identify its influence."[24] Harvard Law professors Zechariah Chafee Jr. and Arthur E. Sutherland advised against use of the Fifth Amendment: "The underlying principle . . . is the duty of the citizen to cooperate in government."[25] The ACLU found the FBI's violations of civil liberties "happily infrequent,"[2] and Schlesinger urged amateur red-hunters to defer to J Edgar Hoover: "We need the best professional counter espionage agency we can get. . . ."[27]

All of this deeply affected the academic world. During the later 'forties and early 'fifties there was a series of investigations of education by every level of government. American colleges and universities emerged with a reputation for having stood up to McCarthyism. The truth is quite different—another instance of the selective memory of the non-Left. How did academics respond to investigations and other pressures?

There were many brave words about academic freedom. Robert Maynard Hutchins of the University of Chicago told the state's Broyles Commission of "the miasma of thought control,"[28] and Harold Taylor's Sarah Lawrence told the Bronxville American Legion that teachers "may not be deprived of any rights they hold as citizens."[29] Charles Seymour of Yale pledged to oppose any "hysterical witch hunt."[30]

Meanwhile, academics were being fired. Those who cooperated with the red hunters were usually safe, but those who did not, especially those who took the Fifth Amendment, were subjected to tremendous pressures by their institutions; those who refused to give in were suspended, censured, or fired. Tenure made no difference. With variations, this was the pattern at—to name a few places—MIT, at Harvard, in the city colleges of New York, in Washington, in California, in Michigan, Colorado, at Rutgers, NYU, and Chicago, at institutions of all sizes and descriptions.[31]

How can this be? How can liberals have spoken out for academic freedom while firing those who tried to assert their freedom? Part of the answer lies in the fact that liberals did not intend for the benefits of academic freedom to apply to *all* academics. Thus, when Harold Taylor spoke of the rights of teachers, he meant those teachers who met the tests of "candor, honesty, and scholarly integrity. . . ." Communists could not meet the tests, and they could neither be given nor retain "the responsibility of membership in the Sarah Lawrence Faculty."[32] At Harvard, President Conant spoke up for academic freedom, while stating that, so far as he knew, there were no Communists there. If there were any, "I hope the Government will ferret them out and prosecute them."[33] Nathan Pusey, who followed him, agreed and stated that Harvard was unalterably opposed to Communism.[34] President Seymour of Yale, and A. Whitney Griswold who followed him, agreed that Communists should not and would not knowingly be appointed to their faculty.[35] At Chicago, Hutchins put the University on record as being "opposed to communism." After all, since the United States government had entrusted Chicago with what Hutchins proudly called "the most momentous military secret in history" (the first chain reaction), the University must be clean. "The faculty number 1,000," said Hutchins; "None of its members is engaged in subversive activities."[36]

What this meant in practice was that the universities protected those who cooperated with the committees and got rid of those who took the Fifth Amendment. This position was sanctioned by the highest authority. In March of 1953 the Association of American Universities adopted a statement which said that membership in the Communist Party "extinguishes the right to a university position," and that it was the duty of professors to cooperate with legislative inquiries, even when they abused their powers ". . . invocation of the Fifth Amendment places upon a professor a heavy burden of proof of his fitness to hold a teaching position and lays upon his university an obligation to re-examine his qualifications for membership in its society." The statement was approved by DuBridge of California Institute of Technology, Kirk of Columbia, Buck of Harvard, Killian of MIT, Miller of Northwestern, Dodds of Princeton, Heald of NYU, Sproul of California, Kimpton of Chicago, Griswold of Yale, and presidents and chancellors of twenty-seven other institutions.[37]

The AAU drew the line between what it called "freedom" and what it called "duty."[38] Just as Hutchins, Taylor, Conant, Seymour, and Griswold had done earlier, it was defining the point at which permissible dissent became impermissible. Truman had done the same with his loyalty order, as did the liberal organizations which had excluded Communists. All of these individuals and groups were engaged in drawing the line. Radicalism, of course, will always be defined by those in positions of power within established institutions as passing over the line. By focusing their activity on drawing the line   rather than opposing the very idea of setting up such a line—these liberals were simply expressing their anti-radicalism, their underlying conservatism.

(There is another sense in which the firings were not at all inconsistent with academic freedom. The term is often misunderstood. What it means, most basically, is the freedom of academics to regulate their own affairs without outside intervention. In this sense, it is like similar freedoms claimed by such professions as law and medicine. These freedoms are thought to help the advancement of the field, and this, in turn, is thought to work in the public interest. The truth may be quite different, as such guilds as the American Medical Association clearly indicate. These fields are extremely hierarchal in their internal government, and each has a self-conscious ideology which sees that hierarchy as necessary and good and which dismisses the possibility of democratic rule as harmful to the field and thus bad for the public.[39] Thus assertions of academic freedom are assertions that final power to make academic decisions should rest with those who rule the profession: they cherish the freedom to clean their own house. Thus the same "academic freedom" which was used as justification for a purge by academic elites is quite correctly used as a sanction against other interferences, such as assertions by students of claims over admissions, curriculum, and hiring, and demands by younger faculty for due process. All of these are indeed interferences with academic freedom.)

The result of all this was a deeply repressive atmosphere, an era of blacklist,[40] a time when academics went to jail for daring to invoke the First Amendment,[41] and the Supreme Court proclaimed the legitimacy of their incarceration.[42] It was no wonder that, in this atmosphere, a man who read of a professor's anti-HUAC activities tried to kill him with a shotgun in his Berkeley office, and succeeded in killing a graduate student.[43] Nor was it any wonder that the students of the 'fifties were called a silent generation. Teachers worried about what their students would say about their lectures and to whom they would say it; they changed their reading lists and grew jumpy about classroom discussions. Some, the American Association of University Professors reported in 1957, began their lectures with statements disclaiming responsibility for any view expressed; "I habitually keep all my classes as confused as possible as to my own views," said one.[44] ("We've never had more freedom," wrote John Roche of Haverford College and the American Civil Liberties Union in 1956.)[45] As they changed their teaching, they changed their writing. So it was that the university was purged of audible radical criticism, and academic thought grew slovenly and stultified in its one-sidedness. If ideas have consequences, all of this was bound to have effects in the world outside the academy.

III. The Ideology of Anti-Radicalism

In those years, American intellectuals were constructing an ideology which said that radicalism was at best an anachronism and that it was both unwise and unnecessary. Reinhold Niebuhr*—whom Walter LaFeber has called the most socially influential American theologian since Jonathan Edwards[46]—spoke out as much against the "illusions" of traditional liberalism as against those of contemporary Communism when he ridiculed "utopian visions of historical possibilities." Rejecting what he called "the heady notion that man is master of his fate and the captain of his soul,"[47] Niebuhr said instead, "Nothing that is worth doing can be achieved in our lifetime. . . ."[48] Isaiah knew that "every desperate effort to establish security will lead to a heightened insecurity." Niebuhr attacked the idea of planning, the "impossible dream" of achieving human happiness, the idea that history could be "rationally ordered." History was uncontrollable and incomprehensible, experience would triumph over dogma, "common sense" over "abstract theories." Condorcet was wrong.[49]

Interestingly, Burke—"the great exponent of the wisdom of historical experience as opposed to the abstract rationalism of the French Revolution"—was right.[50] Niebuhr's liberalism was closer to traditional conservatism: there was no room in it for people who try to make the world over in accord with schemes of what *might be* rather than what *is*.

Arthur M. Schlesinger, Jr., shared Niebuhr's admiration for Burke.[51] Man could not be "reformed by argument" nor

---

* A prominent Protestant theologian active in the affairs of the U.S. Democratic Party.—editor's note

"liberated by a change in economic institutions."[52] "All important problems are insoluble," announced Schlesinger with a certainty that matched Niebuhr at his most lugubrious.[53] Progress and perfectibility were illusions:[54] ". . . the womb has irrevocably closed behind us . . . security is a foolish dream of old men. . . ."[55] Thus history was tragedy, turbulent and unpredictable, beyond human control.[56]

Niebuhr's influence on Schlesinger was clear and was freely acknowledged.[57] Underlying Niebuhr's pessimism was a conception of human nature which Schlesinger also shared. Niebuhr attacked the modern rejection of original sin and asked us instead to reject "Jeffersonian illusions about human nature": the idea of even "*potentially* innocent men" was "an absurd notion."[58] Schlesinger looked with most respect to those doubters and skeptics, men like Freud and Kierkegaard, who had "chart[ed] possibilities of depravity."[59] Schlesinger enlarged the chart: man was at best "imperfect" or "weak"; human experience revealed "anxiety, guilt and corruption"; thee were "dark and subterranean forces in human nature," "fire and treason" in the blood, "aggressive and sinister impulses." Freud had renewed the belief in "the dark, slumbering forces of the will," and the "human love of aggression" which Freud saw, Schlesinger found underlying "all social arrangements."[60]

The darker side of human nature was a fundamental and recurring element in the anti-radical ideology of the 'fifties. Niebuhr and Schlesinger talked about man as they perceived him to have been and assumed that that was the way he must be: that was his *nature*. Leaving aside the question of whether their perception of man in history was correct—it seems to me at best a gross and unsophisticated reading —there remains the question of whether man must in fact b what he has been. These ideologues of the 'fifties answered yes, and this is an almost definitely conservative, Burkean position, buttressed, more recently, by conservative elements in Freud. But this [the question of human nature] is a question for science, and neither Burke nor Freud is science. Science, too, has been as ideological as history, with a strong tendency to document conservative arguments. But we have solid evidence, especially in social psychology, that the idea of "human nature" is itself a myth, that man will kill if his society invites him to and refuse to kill if his society invites him not to; that a man whose chemistry indicates "physiological arousal" will feel himself to be either joyful or furious, depending on what his social context invites him to be; that clinical psychology has severe limits as a predictor of human behavior, since it is a complex interplay between individual variations (which have never been adequately described by clinicians) and social expectations —not the fire and treason in the blood—which determine human behavior. Thus man is, in large part, what society makes him, or allows him to be, and to read his nature back from his conduct in past societies is circular, redundant, and superficial.[61]

With psychology so full of conservative ideology as it has been, from Gustave Le Bon to Freud to the present, it would take great arrogance to say just what human nature is, or even that there is such a thing. Those who did so adhered not to science, but to faith—a kind of dark faith, a mythology about human nature which, as we shall see, was a major element in the anti-radical ideology.

Despite the impossibility of utopia and the insolubility of all problems, America seemed, to Niebuhr and Schlesinger, to have solved most of its problems and to have become "a kind of paradise of domestic security and wealth." Niebuhr fell into what seem somewhat unchristian ecstasies over our "opulence," our movement "toward the ultimate in standards of living," "standards . . . beyond the dreams of avarice of most of the world."[62] Schlesinger felt that anxiety was not a part of most American lives; the quantitative problems had been solved,[63] and there remained, he wrote in *Esquire* in 1960, only "pools of poverty" to be "mopped up."[64] Thus, wrote Niebuhr, we had achieved "social harmony" and "social peace." No wonder a European visitor was so deeply impressed by "The absence of significant social resentments in American life."[65]

This stability, this placidity, was due both to our affluence and to the fact that we had, in Niebuhr's words, "equilibrated power":

> We have attained a certain equilibrium in economic society itself by setting organized power against organized power. When that did not suffice we used the more broadly based political power to redress disproportions and disbalances in economic society.[66]

This idea—that in America government was *not* the instrument of the privileged classes,[67] but rather that it operated so as to equalize the weak and the strong and had succeeded in producing an equilibrium, a consensus —was a central element in the ideology of the 'fifties. It appeared in the work of John Kenneth Galbraith as "the concept of countervailing power"[68] and it pervaded the social science of the era under the name of pluralism.[69] The pluralists envisioned not a power elite, but a multiplicity of elites, of which none is strong enough to dominate. Politics consists of. bargaining, brokerage, compromises among these elites. Daniel Bell wrote: "Democratic politics means bargaining between legitimate groups and the search for consensus."[70] Compromise had been achieved pragmatically and non-ideologically. Those few problems remaining in American society required not ideological but rather technical and non-political solutions.[71] The age of ideology was over: this was the "end of ideology."

The ideology which called itself end of ideology had a very negative view of radicalism and of the participation of masses of people in politics. "The tendency to convert concrete issues into ideological problems, to invest them with moral colour and high emotional charge," wrote Daniel Bell in *Encounter,* "is to invite conflicts which can only damage a society." Fortunately, the two parties competed with each other for power rather than for virtue and had often been indistinguishable in their principles: "the constraining role of the electoral system" was a good thing.[72] Ideological politics disrupted the smoothly functioning system of compromise among informed elites. Such politics were bad, and since social problems could be solved in simpler ways, there was a hint not only of wickedness but also of lunacy about those who felt the need to depart from normal channels. People on the Left tended to see conspiracies about them; they were given to mental disorder, "lonely and frustrated people," said Arthur Schlesinger, Jr., "craving social, intellectual and even sensual fulfillment they cannot obtain in existing society."[73]

Such was the message of the end of ideology, and especially of its leading popularizer, Eric Hoffer, the favourite proletarian philosopher of Dwight Eisenhower, Lyndon Johnson,[74] and Eric Sevareid.[75] Hoffer reduced revolution to psychological aberration.[76] He never stopped to consider the actual grievances that led revolutionaries to frustration. Having denied the substantive reality of the real grievances which have led to revolution, he proceeded to construct a general psychological typology of revolutionaries. In that typology mass movements were interchangeable, since they were composed of the same kinds of people. By this standard, Communists and Nazis, Left and Right, were indistinguishable. Thus, the liberals who adhered to end of ideology saw mass movements as unruly, a threat to stability, and at the same time, conservative or reactionary. The great threat to society came from below, not above, from a tyranny or despotism of the majority, not the minority.[77]

Thus the pluralists saw mass conduct as reactionary, and by complementary reasoning, they saw reactionary conduct as typical of the masses. The Populists of the late nineteenth century were seen as retrogressive, utopian, and anti-semitic. John Roche could write of the South and choose only the lynch mob as an example of "direct democracy."[78] And if the Populists were reactionary, McCarthy was a populist, another excess of democracy. Viewed in the pluralist model, McCarthy's vigilantism was a disruption of the consensus from below, an attempt to impede pluralist politics by an intrusion of grassroots populism. Thus, Leslie Fiedler saw in McCarthy the "sour dregs of populism," "an extension of the ambiguous American impulse toward 'direct democracy' with its distrust of authority, institutions, and expert knowledge. . . ." McCarthy's support came from "the resolutely anti-intellectual small-town weeklies" and from "working-class districts." McCarthy was the inheritor of "the bitterest and most provincial aspects" of an earlier populism.[79]

The ideology described above and the people who expounded it had some fairly specific organizational locations in Americans for Democratic Action, founded in 1947,[80] and in the Congress for Cultural Freedom, founded in 1950.[81] Both organizations were dedicated to the struggle against communism, and their ideology was in part a sanctification of their anti-communism. When the end of ideologist spoke of the pursuit of utopia, it was the USSR that he had in mind; the true believer was a communist. As it turned out, the Congress for Cultural Freedom was underwritten by the

CIA. There *was* a conspiracy, and the very people who were claiming that conspiracies were only activities or fantasies of the Left were at best dupes, at worst liars, hoist on their own petard.[82]

If end of ideology was anti-communist, anti-radical, anti-populist—and CIA ideology to boot—that does not necessarily make it false. The truth may emerge from service to even the worst of patrons. But since we are concerned with the writing of history, and this was an ideology which influenced the writing of history, we must know whether it was in fact true or false. We must, insofar as we can, *test* the end of ideology.

One of the tests of social science is prediction. Without entering into discussion about the possibility of constructing a science of society, we must note that, by any standards, the world of the 'sixties is totally unrecognizeable when seen through the lens of end of ideology. Stability, social harmony, consensus: people in power long for them, but they know that the system which was supposed to provide them has shown its incapacity to do so. Those who do not fit Daniel Bell's definition of "legitimate group" are no longer willing to accept as "democratic politics" a system which excludes them. Foreign visitors no longer marvel at the absence of significant social resentments in America. The events of less than a decade show end of ideology to have been a useless predictor, and this suggests that it was never an adequate description of reality.

Another way of testing end of ideology is to make empirical inquiry into origins of reactionary movements, such as McCarthyism. If the end of ideologists were correct, we would find that such movements have originated from below, not above, from the grass roots rather than from elites, in short, that the evils we have experienced have indeed flowed from an excess of democracy.

I have suggested above that McCarthyism had very

respectable, elite origins. This analysis is confirmed and fully documented in Michael Paul Rogin's excellent study, *The Intellectuals and McCarthy*. First of all, Rogin has tested the pluralists' contention that there was continuity between McCarthy and earlier agrarian radicalism and found it invalid. Testing the contention in the Senator's home state, Wisconsin, Rogin finds entirely different social bases for McCarthy and [Progressive Senator Robert] LaFollette. McCarthy rose on a conservative constituency, the traditional source of Republican strength. Progressivism in Wisconsin "mobilized poor Scandinavian farmers against the richer areas of the state"; McCarthy "rose to power with the votes of the richer German inhabitants of the farms and small cities in southern and eastern Wisconsin. . . ." Those counties which had been Progressive "tended to oppose McCarthy more than other counties in the state."[83] Elsewhere, Rogin finds a similar discontinuity: in North Dakota [Senator] William Langer "had his agrarian radicalism in common with opponents of McCarthy and his McCarthyism in common with opponents of agrarian radicalism." McCarthy did not represent any "new" American Right—just the "old one with new enthusiasm and new power."[84]

In Rogin's analysis, McCarthy emerged from conservative rural politics—which is far from mass politics, but rather the politics of local elites. Thus, for instance, Leslie Fiedler's contention that McCarthy's support by small-town newspapers was an indication that McCarthyism was another movement toward "direct democracy," continuous with Populism, is practically reversed when examined more carefully. Small-town newspapers in fact had an enduring record of opposition to agrarian radicalism; such newspapers are generally the voice of conservative local business interests, and it was these small-town business people who formed a part of McCarthy's base. Thus, Rogin notes, McCarthyism was a movement by a "conservative elite-

—from precinct workers to national politicians. . . ." It "flourished within the normal workings of American politics; not radically outside of them" and was "sustained not by a revolt of the masses so much as by the actions and inactions of various elites."[85]

Thus McCarthyism was more elitist than popular, and it was promoted by a faction within the Republican Party which was more concerned with Communism, Cold War, and Korea than was the country as a whole. *After* these and more liberal elites established communism as an issue, McCarthy jumped on the bandwagon. In power he was supported by moderate Republicans who did not want to split the Party, by conservative and southern Democrats, and by liberal anti-communists who promoted the issue.[86] Thus McCarthy is evidence for the evils of too little democracy, not too much.

The broader implications of Rogin's study have yet to be faced by historians. Mass movements, he concludes, function positively "to overcome the political conservatism" and "the resistance to change among [the] better-educated, better-informed. . . ." Pluralism, which justifies rule by those elites unhampered by popular radicalism, is thus properly seen as "a liberal American venture into conservative political theory."[87]

If we look to the evidence concerning other popular movements, there is much support for Rogin's thesis. In other research, Rogin has found the early support for George Wallace stronger among the middle and upper class than among the working class. "Is 'middle-class authoritarianism' a more fruitful concept than working-class authoritarianism?" he asks.[88] J. David Valaik has examined the attitudes of American Catholics on the Spanish Civil War and has shown that the conclusion that Catholics were pro-Franco is elitist and over-simplified. James Farley, Fulton J. Sheen, Father Coughlin, Senator McCarran, the Knights of Columbus, the Brooklyn *Tablet, Our Sunday Visitor*, and the Holy Name societies—the elite, the hierarchy—yes; but Valaik shows that Roosevelt and machine Democrats erred when they equated the attitudes of "monsignors and diocesan editors" with the attitudes of Catholic laymen, nearly two thirds of whom failed to concur.[89]

The war in Vietnam offers another instructive test for the thesis that the masses are more conservative than elites. We all remember those public opinion polls that Lyndon Johnson carried around in his pocket. Those polls seemed to indicate that the public approved of Johnson's handling of Vietnam, and that whatever pressure came from below favoured greater escalation rather than de-escalation.[90] But, what happened when, instead of asking grossly and simply, "do you approve of President Johnson's handling of the situation in Vietnam?" polls-takers instead presented respondents with a wider range of policy alternatives? The Stanford/NORC [National Opinion Research Corporation] poll (February-March, 1966) found that while sixty-one per cent said that they approved of Johnson, eighty-eight per cent were willing to negotiate with the Vietcong, fifty-four per cent were willing to hold free elections even if the Vietcong might win, and fifty-two per cent were willing to allow a coalition government including the Vietcong. In addition, those opposed to the President were more likely to be "doves" than "hawks."[91] "The country is far ahead of the Administration," wrote the *New York Times*.[92] In other words, when presented with a broader range of policy alternatives than those offered by the vacuous bipartisan politics of the Johnson era, the people chose peace while governing elites conducted war.

The New Hampshire primary of 1968 confirmed the

Stanford Poll and offered another dramatic instance of popular intervention against elite conservatism. A similar intervention had occurred in the anti-war vote of 1952. And in 1964, the electorate had chosen peace and had been over-ruled by an elitist politics which invites usurpation by those in power.[93]

How do we quantify this, and balance it against such data on the other side as the California vote on Proposition 14 [which would have outlawed discrimination in housing] in 1964, the New York vote on a civilian review board [of the police department] in 1966, and all the other referenda with conservative results? I do not know. There would seem, at present, to be no clear basis for a generalization either way. Certainly the data would not justify our moving into a mythic realm of noble workers and unerring electorates. Neither does it justify a complementary mythology about noble elites and the superior trustworthiness of uncommon men. And that is the problem with end of ideology: it asks us to substitute faith for research. Until the research is done, the most conservative of judges will have to conclude that the case for end of ideology is far from proved.

It is possible to construct a program of research which might give us some answers to fundamental questions about the comparative political conduct of elites and masses. To begin with, such a program would *do* research on mass movements. This such pluralist manifestoes as *The New American Right* failed to do.[94] Second, when such research was undertaken, instead of stopping at the point where it detected what it felt to be bad popular conduct, it would, rather than concluding that that was human nature, proceed to ask, why? If lower-class whites throw rocks at blacks, shall we consider our work done when we conclude that lower-class whites are racist, or shall we ask, why? If voters are found to be apathetic, to what extent is that a reflection on them, to what extent a reflection on the choices which the political system offers them? If the public seems to approve of Lyndon Johnson, shall we conclude that they are hawks, or shall we see how they respond to *genuine* alternatives? In each case, the premature conclusion of research betrays a polemicist justifying his faith, not a scientist.

Finally, a sensible program of research on this question would have to apply to the conduct of elites the same standards of criticism which it applies to the conduct of non-elites. To prove the pluralists' case, they must show that referenda produce more conservative results than do legislatures. When they are considering the conservatism of the electorate, they must also consider the Tonkin Bay Resolution, various repressive laws—Smith Acts, McCarran Acts, Mundt-Nixon, the draft and its domestic and foreign effects. If voters can be bought and sold, so can legislatures, and judges, too. Pluralists did an intensive job of exposing what one of them has called the "problematics" of democracy;[95] but they seem entirely to have surrendered their critical sense when it came to the "problematics" of rule by elites. In the absence of such a balanced criticism, what we have is assertion, not evidence, not research but faith—what we might call the anti-democratic faith.[96]

There is clearly about the end of ideology an uncritical admiration of elites, and the ideology finally becomes synonymous with elitism. Only ideologists unquestioningly accepting elitism as if it were objectively valid could have entertained without amazement Daniel Bell's equation of "democratic politics" with bargaining among "legitimate groups."[97] Only the true believer could let pass without a double take such phrases as Irving Kristol's "vulgarization of the democratic idea."[98] The same elitism was there when Arthur Schlesinger, Jr., wrote in *Encounter* "On Heroic Leadership and the Dilemma of Strong Men and Weak Peoples." Schlesinger saw the popular resistance to strong men as rooted in emotion and "envy" of those whom he called "superior persons." The popular fear that "dominant personalities imperiled free institutions" ignored the fact that a strong leader need not be a dictator if his "personal style" embodied democratic values. As an example of such values, Schlesinger quoted Woodrow Wilson:

> The instructed few may not be safe leaders except in so far as they have communicated their instruction to the many, except in so far as they have transmuted their thought into a common, a popular thought. . . . The dynamics of [democratic] leadership lie in persuasion.[99]

Underlying this faith in the instructed few was an attitude of condescension and sometimes scorn of the uninstructed many. Thus Niebuhr noted that there was "no guarantee that poverty will be accompanied by the virtue of humility." If the poor had virtues, that did not mean that their resentments were virtuous: "invariably," they "fail to recognize the root" of "the evils from which they suffer" in themselves and instead "wrongfully assume" that such evils "are solely the consequence of the peculiar malice of their oppressors. . . ."[100] Niebuhr extended this kind of argument into a justification for imperialism, in which the victims seem more to blame than the oppressors. The victims were in fact beneficiaries; had not "imperialism" —he put the word in quotation marks as if it were some native's fantasy —brought technical skills and education? (He also used quotation marks when noting that the industrial world was "white" and the non-technical world was "colored.") A nation such as Indo-China, which was held "in tutelage," became obsessed with "the idea that all of its ills flow from the imperial occupation." "This is never the case," stated Niebuhr with a certainty which seems to contradict the ambiguity which is one of his favourite themes. After all, if the colonial nation was "deficient in capacities for self-government," then "political confusion and economic

chaos" would follow upon "emancipation." Another reason
for delaying decolonization lay in the fact that "few of the
non-industrial nations have sufficiently high standards of
honesty to make democratic government viable." Oriental
culture, he noted, "never inculcated an individual sense of
responsibility to the larger community." Niebuhr's amazing
discussion of Asian character and institutions was, as one
historian put it gently, "not untinged with
condescension."[101]

Perhaps the best comment with which to close a discussion of end of ideology comes from C. Wright Mills:

> If the phrase "the end of ideology" has any meaning at all, it
> pertains to self-selected circles of intellectuals in the richer
> countries. It is in fact merely their own self-image. The total
> population of these countries is a fraction of mankind. . . . To
> speak in such terms of much of Latin-America, Africa, Asia,
> the Soviet bloc is merely ludicrous. Anyone who stands in
> front of audiences—intellectual or mass—in any of these
> places and talks in such terms will merely be shrugged off (if
> the audience is polite) or laughed at out loud (if the audience
> is more candid and knowledgeable). The end-of-ideology is a
> slogan of complacency, circulating among the prematurely
> middle-aged, centered in the present, and in the rich Western
> societies. In the final analysis, it also rests upon a disbelief in
> the shaping by men of their own futures—as history and as
> biography. It is a consensus of a few provincials about their
> own immediate and provincial position.[102]

IV. Historians as Activists: I

What were historians saying in those days? In February of
1953 Daniel J. Boorstin, then at the University of Chicago,
testified before the House Committee on Un-American
Activities, which was investigating Communist methods of
infiltration in education. Boorstin was a cooperative wit-

ness: he brought no lawyer, and he named several people, including two former room-mates, as Communist Party members.[103] He felt that Party members should not be permitted to teach in public schools or in universities. Since he had left the Party, he had been "active" in his opposition to it.[104] How, Representative Moulder asked, had Boorstin expressed his opposition to the Party?[105] Boorstin replied that his opposition had taken two forms: first, "an affirmative participation in religious activities. . . ."[106] The second form of his opposition had been

> an attempt to discover and explain to students in my teaching and in my writing, the unique virtues of American democracy. I have done this partly in my Jefferson book which, by the way, was bitterly attacked in the *Daily Worker* as something defending the ruling classes in America; and in a forthcoming book called *The Genius of American Politics,* which is on the presses at the moment.
>
> I have written articles and book reviews for a commentary [sic] magazine which is a strongly anti-Communist journal. . . .[107]

Later in the hearing, Boorstin was asked whether he had engaged in any other anti-Communist activities since he had come to Chicago in 1944:

> Not that I can recall, sir. I am not basically a political person and I am not active politically. I do feel that the most effective way to fight communism is—the one effective way in which I may have some competence is by helping people to understand the virtues of our institutions and their special values as these emerged from our history, and I have tried to do that.[108]

While taking an aggressive position on one of the central political issues of the day, Boorstin protested that he was not a political person. A year later, Allan Nevins answered the *Saturday Review's* question, "Should American History be

Rewritten?" "Yes."[109] Nevins was especially concerned that "the architects of our material growth—the men like Whitney, McCormick, Westinghouse, Rockefeller, Carnegie, Hill, and Ford" should be granted by historians the enhanced stature which they deserved.[110] We will consider what this meant substantively below. What is of interest at this point is the rationale which Nevins offered:

> The striking shift in our character and our world position in the last half century, of course, has some direct results, already visible, in our interpretation of history. . . .
>
> We may look forward . . . to a more appreciative attitude toward our material strength, and to a more scientific treatment of the factors which have created this material power. In the past our historians were apologetic about this. They condemned our love of the dollar, our race to wealth. . . .
>
> Without denying that some accompaniments of our swift industrialization were atrociously bad we can now assert that this historical attitude was in part erroneous.

Why?

> The nation grew none too fast. We can see today that all its wealth, all its strength were needed to meet a succession of world crises—and we still dwell in a crisis era. Had we applied restrictions to keep our economy small, tame, and timid we would have lost World War I. Had the United States not possessed the mightiest oil industry, the greatest steel industry [etc.] . . . we would indubitably have lost World War II.
>
> Were we significantly weaker today in technical skills, in great mills and factories, and the scientific knowledge which gave us priority with the atomic bomb and hydrogen bomb, all Western Europe would be cowering—we ourselves would perhaps be cowering—before the knout held by the Kremlin. The architects of our material growth . . . will yet stand forth in their true stature as builders, for all their faults, of a

strength which civilization found indispensable.

And in the future, Nevins concluded, historians might say:

> The era in which the United States, summoning all its strength, led democracy in winning the First World War, the Second World War, and the ensuing struggle against the Communist tyranny, was one of the imposing eras of history. It stands invested, in its own fashion, with something of the radiance of the Periclean era, the Elizabethan era, and the era of Pitt and the long struggle against Napoleon.[111]

Little comment is necessary. Nevins explicity related his revisionism to the Cold War. Like Boorstin, Nevins was fighting Communism through history and clearly using the past for contemporary ends. Nevins revelled in contemporary American power and simply asked those on the American side of the Cold War to be more appreciative of the origins of that power. His logic seems inescapable and, I believe, correct. And the converse seems equally true: those who were somewhat more critical of American policy were freer to see the past more clearly.[112]

In his 1950 Presidential Address to the American Historical Association, entitled "Faith of an Historian," Samuel Eliot Morison had seemed at times to endorse an activist role for the historian.[113] The historian "should feel a sense of responsibility to his public" and "he will inevitably try to answer some of the questions that contemporary society asks of the past. . . ." But Morison made it clear that he meant this quite differently from the way Charles Beard, the debunkers and the dialectical materialists meant it. Beard had probably contributed "more than any other writer, except Henry L. Mencken, to the scornful attitude of intellectuals toward American institutions, that followed World War I." Some of Beard's writing was closer to "imprecatory preaching" than to "history in the accepted, traditional sense of the word"; he was a good example for young historians "of what happens when a historian consciously writes to shape the future instead of to illuminate the past. . . ."[114] History had to be written with a proper balance—*mesure*, Morison called it. In its absence he saw the historiographical situation as "unbalanced and unhealthy, tending to create a sort of neoliberal stereotype." Although professing himself to be something of a Jeffersonian, Morison saw the need for "a United States history written from a sanely conservative point of view. . . ." The historian, Morison warned, "owes respect to tradition and to folk memory . . . historians, deal gently with your people's traditions!" Beard and others had "ignored wars, belittled wars, taught that no war was necessary and no war did any good, even to the victor." Morison thus held historians largely responsible for youth's "spiritual unpreparedness" for World War II: they "should have pointed out that war does accomplish something, that war is better than servitude. . . ." The years from 1920 to 1940 were "two woeful decades" when historians were "robbing the people of their heroes, . . . insulting their folk-memory of great figures whom they admired. . . ." In doing this, the historians had "repelled men of good will and turned other men, many not of good will, to Communism."[115]

While attacking Beard's present-mindedness, Morison had argued for the claims of heroic tradition as against historical truth, had held those historians less respectful than himself of those traditions responsible for turning people to Communism, and had offered, to boot, a precise academic translation of the slogan, "better dead than red." It is another measure of the present-mindedness of the profession that no one seems to have noticed the ludicrousness of an admiral wrapping himself in the mantle of objectivity while haranguing his audience on the glories of war and the evils of pacifism.[116]

In the *Harvard Guide to American History*, Morison expressed himself more bluntly, urging the historian to avoid a " 'smart aleck' attack on popular beliefs. . . ."[117] He also delineated more specifically the activist role which he saw as appropriate for the historian.[118] The historian, he said, should be "active and vigorous" and should find ways to make himself "solid" in his community. Some of these ways were: delivering centennial and founders' day speeches, addressing clubs, lodges, and patriotic societies, and providing data for anniversary pageants and broadcasts. The historian should cooperate with "patriotic and ancestral societies such as the Colonial Dames, Daughters of the American Revolution, and Daughters of the Confederacy instead of regarding them (however strong the provocation) as natural enemies."[119]

Others were finding ample reason *not* to cooperate with the D.A.R. (Daughters of the American Revolution). Morison's politics are his own affair, but it is undeniable that he *has* politics. He exhorts to an activism which favours, rather than opposes, the traditions which he admires. He invites the historian to support patriotic societies and celebrations, but not to support communists, nor socialists, nor even civil rights or labor. The instruction to become "solid" with the community in one which, by definition, bars radical activity. Morison's partisanship is clear, and his exclusions clearly draw the line between what is appropriate and inappropriate activism for the historian. It is incontestable that he is endorsing activism, so long as it is of the appropriate sort.

Elsewhere in the *Harvard Guide*, Morison spoke on another aspect of activism. The historian, he said, "should have frequent recourse to the book of life." Those who had fought in wars, for instance, could "read man's doings in the past with far greater understanding than if they had spent these years in sheltered academic shades."[120] Similar words came at about the same time from a younger Harvard historian, Arthur Schlesinger, Jr. "American historians," he said, "spend too much time writing about events which the whole nature of their lives prevent them from understanding. Their life is defined by universities, libraries and seminars . . . I gained more insight into history from being in the war and working for the government than I did from my academic training."[121] That Schlesinger's experience in government informed and enlivened his writing there is no doubt, and Morison's experiences at sea and elsewhere did the same for his writing. But this is not simply a question of literary art. It is again a question of politics. The profession endorses the activism of a Democratic Party politician, the activism of an admiral and official naval historian. But the profession is hardly ready to endorse and admire the involvement of those who actively oppose the admirals and the party politicians, the veterans of the anti-wars. Ask yourself: would Arthur Mann have written admiringly of Staughton Lynd, as he has of Arthur Schlesinger, Jr., that he "writes history as he votes and votes as he writes. To a spectatorial age his ardent commitment to a cause has been a salutary countervailing tendency. [Schlesinger writes] . . . from the inside, with life, color, passion, drama, and conviction."[122] Certain convictions are seen as aiding scholarship, others are seen as interfering with it. In that distinction the profession expresses its ideology and its politics.

Perhaps the Sameul Eliot Morison Prize for *mesure* should go to the A.H.A. Presidential Address which preceded his. In 1949 Conyers Read spoke on "The Social Responsibilities of the Historian." He set out to define "the responsibilities of those who disseminate history, to those whose pattern of the past is one of the most important factors in their present behavior and in their future plans and hopes.'' The Communists, the Nazis, and others had their versions of history. "What part,'' Read asked, "are we as historians to play in what everybody is calling education for democracy?'' The experience of the preceding twenty-five years had shown that words were weapons: "Dr. Goebbels understood that, Mr. Molotov understands it.'' It was too late in world history for neutrality. This meant that historians must "recognize certain fundamental values as beyond dispute." They must carry back into their scrutiny of the past "the same faith in the validity of our democratic assumptions which, let us say, the astronomer has in the validity of the Copernican theory.'' And what if the past turned up data which seemed to question these assumptions?

> We shall still, like the doctor, have to examine social pathology if only to diagnose the nature of the disease. But we must realize that not everything which takes place in the laboratory is appropriate for broadcasting at the street corners.

The call for suppression was integrated into the demand that historians declare war on the Soviet Union:

> Confronted by such alternatives as Mussolini and Hitler and last of all Stalin have imposed, we must clearly assume a militant attitude if we are to survive. The antidote to bad doctrine is better doctrine, not neutralized intelligence. We must assert our own objectives . . . and organize all the forces of our society in support of them. Discipline is the essential prerequisite of every effective army whether it march under the Stars and Stripes or under the Hammer and Sickle . . . Total war, whether it be hot or cold, enlists everyone and calls upon everyone to assume his part. The historian is no freer from this obligation than the physicist . . .

> This sounds like the advocacy of one form of social control
> as against another. In short, it is.[123]

Let Irwin Unger speak of political neutrality; Conyers Read knew better. The message from Read and the rest was activist, militant, and anti-radical, urging rewriting and suppression.[124]It is wrong to think of the historians of the 'fifties as engaged in "passionless research." John Higham, to whom we are indebted for the first general critiques of consensus history, was perhaps too close to the events that he was describing to see that the American celebrationists were in fact quite passionate men, intensely committed, with a moral vision of their own. It is not true, as Higham wrote, that such handbooks as the *Harvard Guide* "ignored" "moral evaluation." Nor is it true that scholarship was moving towards a "moral vacuum." While Higham was urging the historian to be a "moral critic," that is precisely what these passionate and committed historians were doing, renovating the entire American past in a veritable riot of present-mindedness, in defiance of all historiographical law and order.[125]

V. American History Rewritten [126]

Writing in 1958, Daniel J. Boorstin described the American colonies as "a disproving ground for utopias."[127] Massachusetts succeeded because the Puritans were a practical people who "resisted the temptation of utopia"; they were "concerned less with the ends of society than with its organization and less with making the community good than with making it effective . . ."[128] Boorstin's non-ideological Puritans were indeed effective: they built a strong and homogeneous society and maintained that homogeneity by excluding those who did not agree with them; when that did not work, they killed them. Just as Boorstin says, intolerance was a "source of strength."[129]

The Quakers were the special victims of that intolerance. What might seem to some a moving and heroic story of a quest for religious liberty is, for Boorstin, little more than a tale of true believers getting their just deserts. The Quakers were engaged in a "Quest for Martyrdom." Boorstin finds their appetite for suffering insatiable and ridicules their "bizarre and dauntless spirit": "Never before perhaps have people gone to such trouble or travelled so far for the joys of suffering for their Lord . . . Never was a reward sought more eagerly than the Quakers sought out their crown of thorns."[130] Thus Boorstin ignores the substance of what the Quakers suffered for, reduces their struggle to sickness, and sacrifices them to a higher value than freedom: consensus and social stability. The ideological challenge must not be allowed to weaken the pragmatic society.

In Pennsylvania, where the Quakers ruled, their tolerance was a source of weakness: non-Quakers "poured in," until the Quakers were in the minority. Thus Boorstin dismisses Pennsylvania as a failure, which it certainly was, if your ideal is a stable, homogeneous society, free of dissent. The Quakers also failed because of the "uncompromising obstinacy" with which they held to their beliefs. Theirs was "the curse of perfectionism," and they spoke to the 1950's as an "example of the futility of trying to govern by absolutes."[131]

Boorstin ridicules Quaker policy toward the Indians and quotes with approval Benjamin Franklin's more hawkish line: "I do not believe we shall ever have a firm peace with the Indians till we have well drubbed them." Boorstin dismisses as "unrealistic" and "inflexible" Quaker policies which built on the insistence that Indian grievances were rooted in abuse by the English. The Quakers failed to understand "the character of these unfamiliar people"; their view of the Indian was based on "false premises about human nature." To reject someone else's ideas about human nature as false, one must have ideas of one's own. In this instance, Boorstin is saying either that the Indians' "character" was inferior or that "human nature" is in some inherent sense evil. Neither case is proved, and in this context, the argument amounts to an apology for genocide.[132]

In describing the failure of Georgia, Boorstin offers persuasive evidence that planning for the colony was unrealistic. But his conclusion goes somewhat beyond his evidence: no plan made in Europe could fit America. Thus the focus shifts from the specifics of the plan for Georgia to the idea of planning itself, and this broader focus gives meaning to the terms which Boorstin uses to describe the colony's failure: "London Blueprint for Georgia Utopia," "Death of a Welfare Project." The present-mindedness of all this is undeniable: just as it was "extravagant" for the trustees of Georgia to attempt to master the new world, it is unrealistic and utopian for men today to think that they can, by the application of reason, master a hostile environment.[133]

In Boorstin's pessimistic view of human nature and of human possibilities, we may find more than a hint of Reinhold Niebuhr. Indeed, it should be clear that Boorstin's view of early America has much in common with the outlook of the anti-communist ideologues of the 'fifties described above. In addition to the distinctly Niebuhrian views just mentioned, we have detected end of ideology, the dangers of ideology, of radicalism, and even of dissent.[134] This is, as we have noted above, a distinctly Burkean complex. In the second volume of *The Americans*, while approving of Burke, Boorstin condemns his great radical adversary, Tom Paine, in Burkean terms. Paine's *Common Sense*, says Boorstin (contrasting it with John Adams'

Thoughts on Government) was "crude," "hardly a profound or durable theory of government," a propagandistic amalgam of "simples and absolutes."[135] The unfavourable picture of Paine as the archetypal radical, proposing utopian schemes and trying to make the world over from a blueprint, was most fully developed in Cecelia M. Kenyon's "Where Paine Went Wrong."[136] Here Paine is described as the "Peter Pan of the Age of Reason," a "prophet," a "crusader." Rather than looking to experience, Paine derived his principles from "preconceived" ideals; "He reasoned from first principles, normative principles. . . ."; "Logic and Reason were his guides. . . ." We know from Burke just how harmful all this is, and there is no essential disagreement between Kenyon and Burke. The key to Paine's unrealism is his failure to understand human nature. There is, says Kenyon, a "dark side of human nature" which the "immature" Paine was unable to see.[137]

Kenyon's Paine was a man of "zeal" and "devotion" who was "quite prepared to renounce his life. . . ." She suggests that politics was a form of therapy for him, a way in which he "'found himself,'" expressing his "profoundest urge . . .": "His was an all-or-none temperament, and he was happiest when he devoted his all to a noble cause."[138] This complex is familiar to readers of Eric Hoffer. Writing in 1951 — the same year that *The True Believer* was published — Kenyon got there without Hoffer's help: the ideas were in the air.[139]

The attack on Paine is also an attack on communism. Forrest McDonald, like Reinhold Niebuhr,[140] identified the two pejoratively.[141] And, to Kenyon, Tom Paine writing *Common Sense* is equated with Karl Marx writing *The Communist Manifesto*: both are utopian, unrealistic, simplistic.[142]

Stanley Elkins' abolitionists are also true believers, and Elkins' portrayal of the society in which they moved is strongly influenced by pluralism, consensus, and end of ideology.[143] Elkins asks, as had the abolitionists, what is the best way to deal with institutionalized social problems? He answers that those committed to institutions and sensitive to them are best equipped to deal with them. In order fully to understand institutions —and thus to know how to subvert them —the intellectual must have "some sort of daily orientation to institutions. . . ." I can think of a fairly specific daily orientation to bad institutions: opposition. But for Elkins, daily orientation seems to be synonymous with membership and endorsement. Thus, a man such as Thomas Jefferson was well equipped to deal with slavery because his "mind operated under the balanced tensions created not only by a repugnance to the system but also by a commitment to it." "Our best social thinking occurred" in the late 1780's because "men with specific stakes in society, men attached to institutions and with a vested interest in one another's presence, men aware of being engaged with concrete problems of power" were writing and debating.[144] We might well ask where such an analysis leaves those *opposed* to the system, especially those who come to their opposition in what are, after all, among the most frequent ways, as non-members and non-beneficiaries, people *without* specific stakes.

By the 1830's those in America's intellectual centre "had no close commitment to any of society's institutions," and thus they were "men without responsibility."[145] The Transcendentalists were

> men without connections. Almost without exception, they had no ties with the sources of wealth; there were no lawyers nor jurists among them; none of them ever sat in a government post; none was a member of Congress; they took next to no part in politics at all. . . . Not one of them wielded even the limited influence of a professor. . . .[146]

The charitable reader might suppose that powerlessness is in itself enough of a cross to bear, but Elkins condemns abolitionists and intellectuals for having "no vested interest," for their opposition to "the system," to the church, to businessmen as a class, to the government, and the poll tax, to political parties, indeed to "the Constitution itself."[147] In all this, there seems not the vaguest realization that, under certain circumstances, such institutions might indeed be worthy of opposition. Is it *prima facie* ridiculous to oppose businessmen as a class? Is it simply a manifestation of deep guilt for Emerson to describe the pervasiveness of the evils of the business society: "by coming out of trade you have not cleansed yourself. The trail of the serpent reaches into all the lucrative professions and practices of man. Each has its own wrongs."[148] Is it ludicrous for an anti-slavery movement to speak against political parties which countenance slavery, and is it ludicrous for such a movement to see the Constitution as protecting slavery, and thus to oppose it? Describing Thoreau's refusal to pay a poll tax without relating his act to the Mexican War is like describing the tearing and public burning of small scraps of paper in the 1960's without mentioning draft cards or Vietnam. Thoreau's conduct brings Elkins to an almost Boorstinian ire against the dissenter, with a suggestion of unpatriotism: it was the very state against which Thoreau was protesting which had allowed him to contemplate alternatives; "Could he have foreseen it, this might well have confounded Theodore Parker's grandfather, who had commanded the militia on Lexington Green."[149]

If one starts with the assumption that institutions are, *per se*, good, and one is thenceforth unwilling to examine the *substance* of criticisms of specific institutions, this is simply to say that one starts with the assumption that those who attack institutions are, by definition, wrong. This is an anti-radical assumption: by ignoring the substance of the radical critique, it assumes that substance has nothing to do with the critique. This *is* Elkins' assumption, and it is part of a generalized assault upon reformers, whose motives are seen as irrational. Thus Elkins asserts that "in the history of American reform no direct connection can be found between the extent of a given social evil and the intensity of the reform activity directed against it." (One wonders how well *institutional* politics would stand up to such a test.) Guilt is the irrational force which has driven American reformers; the lack of a confession box seems to play a major role.[150]

The abolitionist is, then, like Hoffer's true believer, the man driven by a "fever" to a "root-and-branch solution." He is, again like the true believer, very similar to his adversary at the other extreme of the political spectrum: in the years before the Civil War, "polar opposites" in North and South both expressed themselves with "a simple moral severity."[151] It perhaps tells us more about the 1950's than about the 1850's that there were writers in the recent decade who cited attacks on social horrors and evaluated them primarily as reflecting the psychological defects of the men who uttered the words. Finally, abolitionists, too, are surrogate Communists, especially in their use of such allies as John Quincy Adams, whom Elkins describes as "the very prince of fellow travelers."[152]

A decade before Elkins' *Slavery*, Arthur M. Schlesinger, Jr., had published a brief but influential article entitled "The Causes of the Civil War: A Note on Historical Sentimentalism."[153] Although the essay's present-mindedness seems not to have been noticed at the time, it was, among other things, a justification for the Cold War. Credit is due to Schlesinger: the essay represented a real advance over the interpretation of the Civil War which it attacked, and since that advance was in what seemed a humane direction, the underlying acceptance of the necessity of the Cold War was missed.

Schlesinger's essay was a response to such Civil War "revisionists" as James G. Randall and Avery Craven, who had argued that that war was "needless" and "repressible" and could have been avoided had it not been for a "blundering generation" of politicians. Schlesinger correctly noted that the revisionists had to demonstrate that a nonblundering generation could indeed have achieved a peaceful solution—without preserving slavery.[154] Schlesinger argued persuasively that the revisionists could provide no such demonstration.[155] A generation of young historians — including this one[156]—greeted with enthusiasm what they took to be Schlesinger's central message: slavery *was* a moral issue, and the claim that it could have been resolved but for blundering amounts to an apology for slavery, or at least to an excuse for its preservation.

Some of us took Schlesinger's argument as implying an attack on the idea that the abolitionists were meddlers, troublemakers, fanatics and neurotics who refused to let things work themselves out. In fact, Schlesinger accepted without argument the contention that the abolitionists *were* "neurotics and fanatics." Although he differed with the revisionists in seeing the rise of the abolitionist challenge as "inevitable," he was by no means convinced of the abolitionists' virtue and indeed suspected that "people who indulge in criticism of remote evils may not be so pure of heart as they imagine. . . ."[157]

But if Schlesinger was more in agreement with the revisionists on the nature of the abolitionists than might at first have appeared, his disagreement with them about the Civil War, and war in general, was nonetheless fundamental. Schlesinger's critique of the revisionists seems to make good sense as an analysis of the causes of the Civil War. But the essay was more than that. Schlesinger described the slavery problem as "peculiarly recalcitrant." To say that the problem had a solution short of war was to engage in "broad affirmations of faith: if only the conflict could have been staved off long enough, then somehow, somewhere, we could have worked something out." Such an attitude, said Schlesinger, raised questions which went beyond the narrow question of the causes of the Civil War: "the whole modern view of history"—of which Civil War revisionism was only one part—was characterized by "optimistic sentimentalism." Schlesinger saw in Randall "a touching afterglow of the admirable 19th century faith in the full rationality and perfectibility of man. . . ." But "the experience of the 20th century has made it clear that we gravely overrated man's capacity to solve the problems of existence within the terms of history." Expounding on another 'fifties theme, Schlesinger stated that a more realistic awareness of "human nature" would bring us to accept "the unhappy fact . . . that man occasionally works himself into a logjam, and . . . the logjam must be burst by violence." The revisionist view expressed a "characteristically sentimental conception of man and of history." The truth of the matter was that "Man is generally entangled in insoluble problems; history is consequently a tragedy in which we are all involved, whose keynote is anxiety and frustration, not progress and fulfillment. . . ." "All important problems are insoluble . . . ," Schlesinger had written at the same time in *The Vital Center*.[158]

Sentimentality, tragedy, the depravity of human nature, man's inability to control history: these were the central themes of Schlesinger's political writings at the time, and they were also the central message of his essay on the Civil War. He subtitled the essay, "A Note on Historical Sentimentalism." The term "sentimentalism" appears frequently in his writings on contemporary affairs, and there the word has a fairly precise meaning. Schlesinger shared Niebuhr's critique of "sentimental optimism"; the "sentimentalists," Schlesinger wrote in *The Vital Center*, were one with "the utopians, the wailers"; it was a "sentimental belief in progress" which was at the core of what Schlesinger called "Doughface Progressivism." At about the same time that he wrote of the Civil War, elsewhere Schlesinger was worried about the progressive, the "fellow traveler," "softened up . . . for Communist permeation and conquest" by his "sentimentality." In Schlesinger's vocabulary, "sentimentalism" was an expression of contempt, emerging from a Burkean complex, and used especially to describe those who hoped for a solution to the Cold War short of hot war.[159]

Schlesinger's Soviet Union was—like the old South—a slave system, a totalitarian society, in which totalitarianism was intensifying rather than moderating as time passed. In the South, the reaction to abolitionism produced "the extinction of free discussion" which meant "the absolute extinction of any hope of abolition through internal reform": "With the book-burning, the censorship of the mails, the gradual illegalization of dissent, the South was in the process of creating a real machinery of repression in order more effectively 'to defend its existence.'"[160] (Interestingly, while Schlesinger seemed to accept the idea that the closing down of Southern society was, at least in part, a response to outside hostility, he ridiculed the idea that the Soviet Union was "surrounded by capitalist aggressors" and saw instead "a conspiratorial paranoia," "the psychoses of totalitarianism").[161]

"A society closed in the defense of evil institutions thus creates moral differences far too profound to be solved by compromise." So wrote Schlesinger of the South. His writings in the years after World War II said the same things of the Soviet Union. The differences between the U.S. and the U.S.S.R. were uncompromiseable: the U.S. must surrender neither "military strong points" nor "standards and values."[162] Conceding the value of Schlesinger's interpretation of the Civil War—clearly, his convictions informed his scholarship—we must still ask whether it is legitimate to generalize from the Civil War to the Cold War and to wars in general. If the Civil War revisionists were wrong, does that mean that the revisionists of more recent wars are also wrong? To say so is to impose assumptions about history and human nature on the data rather than to let the generalizations flow from the data. Argument that slavery was central to a thus unavoidable Civil War is not evidence that the First World War was unavoidable, a war for democracy. Argument that the Civil War was a struggle between slavery and freedom is not evidence for a similar polarization in descriptions of the Soviet Union and the United States in the twentieth century.

Schlesinger's position had a great deal in common with Admiral Morison's call, at about the same time, for historians to take a more positive attitude toward war than had Charles A. Beard. Morison's attack on revisionism aimed at the same attitudes toward war which lay behind the Civil War revisionists whom Schlesinger criticized. Schlesinger replaced Morison's brassy militarism with an apparent fatalism, more in tune with the ideology of the 'fifties. A busy activist for an aggressive policy, Schlesinger somberly announced that things, not men, were in control, and we must be prepared to accept the consequences of our inability to control history. Schlesinger's "note on historical sentimentalism" was a retroactive declaration of the conclusions to which the Cold War had brought him.

While Boorstin, Kenyon, Elkins and others were putting earlier American radicals on the psychiatrist's couch, the same treatment was being applied to the Populists. Oscar Handlin, Richard Hofstadter and others were developing a new and distinctly unfavourable view in which a movement previously thought radical and progressive exposed an underside: retrogressive and utopian, anti-semitic, nativist, and irrational. Adopting this view, the end of ideologists also linked a deplorable past to an unpleasant present. Populism became a precursor of McCarthyism. In various writings, Norman Pollack attempted to restore the picture of the Populists as progressive, not retrogressive. Taking a new look at the human cost of industrialization in this country, Pollack found the Populists' vision clear and their critique sound. The Populists responded to real, not imagined, oppressions. "What stands out about the Populist mind," wrote Pollack in his "Fear of Man," "is an affirmation of man, a faith in man's capability to shape his own history."[163]

Why, then, Pollack asked, "did historians embark on the denigration of Populism, and why did the recent interpretation gain such widespread acceptance?" If an affirmation of man was at the heart of Populism, Pollack concluded, the attack on Populism expressed a fear of man. Pollack saw this attack as part of a general rejection of radicalism in the American past. The celebration of consensus meant the rejection of any disturbance to the *status quo*, and thus the rejection of social protest and striving to make the world over. In all of this, Pollack saw an extreme present-mindedness: historians were using research about the origins of authoritarianism as "a shield to hide behind while reading current biases into the past." And the present-day values which were preoccupying these historians were the outgrowth of the Cold War and McCarthyism. More precisely, they *were* McCarthyism. The rejection of Populism constituted a capitulation to McCarthyism and an identification with it: "the consensus framework and McCarthyism" were "actually one and the same underlying trend."[164]

The suggestion that a school of historians which thought itself primarily liberal was in fact McCarthyite won Pollack few friends among historians. Oscar Handlin accused him —along with other defenders of Populism—of Manichaeanism, befogging the issue, and "glaring . . . failure of analysis."[165] Irwin Unger saw in Pollack's language "the verbal small change of twentieth century academic radicalism" and originated his charge of "inadmissible present-mindedness."[166] Pollack had in fact offered a brilliant analysis, the first major step by an historian towards an understanding of the contemporary meaning of consensus and pluralism as conservative politics. Pollack's earlier insights have been confirmed by Rogin, who, as we have seen, shows discontinuity between Populism and McCarthyism and has described the conservative and elitist content of pluralism.[167] In the context of the present analysis, the attack on Populism can be clearly seen as but another front in the end of ideologists' war on the "sentimentalists," those who did not share the anti-democratic faith, those who asserted that man could indeed make his own history, those who refused to accept social stability as a definition of democracy.

While Populist stock was falling among historians, the stock of their adversaries, the Robber Barons, was rising. We have noted above the Cold War rationale offered by Allan Nevins for a more appreciative attitude toward these "architects of our material growth" (not "Robber Barons," said Nevins; Arthur Schlesinger agreed).[168] Nevins practiced what he preached: his doctrine was reflected in his admiring biography of John D. Rockefeller.[169] Noting that "Our Industrial Revolution cost us . . . infinitely less than Russia's," Nevins reminded the reader that but for our swift industrialization, "the free world" might have lost World

Wars I and II.[170] Thirteen years before, Nevins had published another biography of Rockefeller. Although Rockefeller had clearly emerged as a hero of American enterprise, the earlier Nevins had found grounds for criticism of some of his methods. Nevins had rationed his criticism, but he could not avoid some of it when he described Rockefeller's labour policies. He offered evidence that Rockefeller employed labour spies, and concluded:

> . . . the liberal activities of John D. Rockefeller, Jr., in promoting the industrial representation system in various of the former Standard companies, indicate that numerous employees became discontented with the paternalistic system.[171]

Here is the same sentence as it appears in the 1953 edition:

> . . . the liberal activities of John D. Rockefeller, Jr., in promoting the industrial representation system in various of the former Standard companies, *opened a new era in labor relations*.[172]

The transformation seems worthy of a Soviet Encyclopedia. Something which is evidence in 1940 of some dissatisfaction on labour's part is converted, in 1953, into a feat of industrial statesmanship. Herbert Aptheker pointed out the discrepancy between the two editions in 1954, but no one was listening.[173]

The title of Nevins' 1953 biography, *Study in Power,* reflected the 'fifties historians' rising admiration for the powerful rather than the powerless. Rockefeller the businessman was the beneficiary of this admiration, and so were leaders in general. Michael Rogin has described a shift in Richard Hofstadter's attitude toward leadership. In 1948 Hofstadter felt that it was safer that the public be "overcritical" of its leaders rather than "overindulgent" towards them; seven years later he focused on the dangers of the overcritical attitude, the popular suspicion of power.[174] The same Nevins who admired Rockefeller's power wrote in the *New York Times* that "a nation without leadership is a rudderless ship." He saw in our system of checks and balances defects as well as virtues: the "fear of unrestrained power, of dictatorial tendencies" had led the Founding Fathers to place "obstacles" in the way of political leadership.[175] We have seen similar attitudes in Arthur Schlesinger, Jr.'s admiration of "Heroic Leadership."

The desire for strong political leadership focused on the office of the President, and the area of his powers which drew historians' greatest attention was the making of foreign policy. Schlesinger wrote of strong men and of the instructed few and, as he read the record of American history, it seemed to him that the "temporary devolution of power" from the legislature to the president during wartime "can take place without permanent harm to democratic institutions."[176] This ideology generally combined a distrust of the people with a feeling that the Constitution had been made for a simpler time and was not adequate to the exigencies of decision-making in the atomic age. The complexities of the modern era required quick, centralized, secret decisions. One of those who expressed those attitudes most forcefully was Thomas A. Bailey, who wrote in 1948,

> . . . because the masses are notoriously short-sighted, and generally cannot see danger until it is at their throats, our statesmen are forced to deceive them into an awareness of their own long-run interests. . .
>
> Deception of the people may in fact become increasingly necessary, unless we are willing to give our leaders in Washington a freer hand. In the days of the horse and buggy we could jog along behind our billowy barriers with relative impunity, but in the days of the atomic bomb we may have to move more rapidly than a lumbering public opinion will

permit . . . the yielding of some of our democratic control of foreign affairs is the price that we may have to pay for greater physical security.[177]

Early in 1951, the United States was at war in Korea. Harry Truman had sent troops to Asia without congressional authorization. As Senator Robert A. Taft saw it, the President had "usurped" power and violated the Constitution. A Republican congressman introduced a resolution requiring that congress give formal authorization before any American troops could be sent out of the country in the future.[178] Henry Steele Commager offered a partisan defense of Truman's conduct in two articles in the *New York Times Magazine*.[179] To Commager, the issue seemed hardly worth discussing: the principles involved in the assault on presidential power "had no support in law or in history."[180] The constitutional issue had been settled time and again, clearly in favour of presidential power: "It is so hackneyed a theme that even politicians might reasonably be expected to be familiar with it."[181] After he had offered his constitutional documentation, Commager turned to history and found "no basis in our own history for the distrust of the Executive authority." Such distrust proceeded "not out of real but out of imagined dangers. It is rooted not in experience but in fears." The assault on the executive power was "dangerous."[182] It could lead to a substitution for the Presidential system of "a bastard product of Presidential and parliamentary. . ." which would "destroy the constitutional fabric of the Republic." And to tie the President's hands under conditions of modern warfare was to "invite aggression."[183]

Commager, Nevins, and others were obviously, to borrow a phrase from Irwin Unger, "projecting onto history" their "present cold war fears and frustrations." Commager had justified the presidential power to send troops to Asia without congressional authorization. All of this led quite directly to Vietnam —to a legitimization of executive usurpation, decision-making without the involvement of the people or their representatives —and official lying.[184]

A persistent theme of the period was an interest in "American Character." Those who wrote on the subject expressed themselves with confidence and largely uncritically. Underlying the quest for an American Character were certain assumptions which constituted a political ideology. To describe a national character generally meant to assume uniqueness and a high degree of unity, consensus, classlessness, lack of conflict. The portrait of the national character thus drawn defined evidence of disunity, conflict, class as of secondary importance, if indeed it was acknowledged that there was such evidence. In other words, the national character as described was an expression of pluralism and, as such, it excluded blacks, the poor, radicals. Consider, as one example of many, the class and racial assumptions implicit in Henry Steele Commager's generalization that America is "a paradise for children."[185]

This ideology was institutionalized in the new field of American Studies, which thought of itself as a "movement" and added to the college curriculum courses rich in ideological content.[186] Some of the field's central themes were reflected in such books as David M. Potter's *People of Plenty*, which parodied socialism while constructing a theory of American Character on the contention that "a thousand measurements of our . . . plenty" indicated that abundance was "a basic condition of American life."[187]

All of this, as I have indicated above, made for poor social science, if prediction is a measure of social science. And the end-of-ideology historians did not hesitate to make predictions. In the area of foreign policy, Henry Steele Commager saw few, "outside of Russia and her satellites," looking with misgivings on the prospect that America should "control the course of world history in the second half of the twentieth century."[188] Looking ahead to 1970, he foresaw a decreased military budget and a pooling of resources by "the more affluent peoples of the Western Hemisphere" in order "to help the peoples and nations of Asia, Africa and Latin America."[189] Looking further ahead, toward a "Brave World of the Year 2000," Commager foresaw a United States expanding and perfecting "the role which it so generously assumed when it launched the historic Marshall Plan." By 2000, he said, America could be, "to the new worlds of Asia and Africa and Latin America, what Athens and Rome were to the peoples of the ancient world, what England and Holland and France were to the Western world of the seventeenth to nineteenth centuries."[190] This was all seen within the context of benevolence, without power or military connotations. And for those who were worried about a militarized America, Arthur Schlesinger, Jr., offered reassurance: "There is no evidence of the development of a unified military position on political questions," he wrote in 1949; "the appearance of generals in public life at this time is due as much as anything to the fact that they are men of ability, exempt from partisan criticism and used to working for the government at a low rate of pay."[191]

In the area of domestic prophecy, we have already noted Schlesinger's prediction of an end to poverty once those few remaining pools were "mopped up." (Earlier, Schlesinger had seen in Herbert Hoover's 1928 vision of the imminent end of poverty "the smugness of that incredible decade").[192] As for the racial situation, Schlesinger saw this as largely a Southern matter and he was optimistic: ". . . the South on the whole accepts the objectives of the civil rights program as legitimate, even though it may have serious and intelligible reservations about timing and method.''[193] Commager foresaw progress in race relations and in education, public health and conservation, and further movement toward a classless society.[194] In 1959, Allan Nevins foresaw similar gains and constructed a dialogue in which Booker T. Washington looked at 1970 and found it good:

> "What strikes me most . . . is the remarkable rise in the homogeneity of the population. So many city people have moved to Scarsdales, Newton Centers, Bryn Mawrs and farther out. . . . So many women have moved into offices and the professions that the sex line is blurred, too. . . . Social mobility remains high.
>
> But the great gain is the Negro's. So many have moved into the North and West, so many have gotten into industry on the same assembly lines with whites, so many have pushed into business and lately even the professions, that the color line begins to blur, too."

"You mean," Nevins had Emerson remark, "that whereas the country used to be a medley, now in 1970 people begin to regard themselves as all Americans together."[195]

The leading non-Left historians in the period since World War II have, as Unger said of the New Left, "confuse[d] the truths of the past with the needs of the present and future." It is simply ludicrous to speak of these men as "politically neutral." Nonetheless, present-mindedness is not all bad, and the activist historians of the 'fifties might take some consolation from the words of Staughton Lynd, an activist of the Left, who has written, in defense of present-mindedness, *"Wie es eigentlich gewesen** is an elephant with many sides, and if a scholar grasps that leg which is closest to him he nevertheless lays hold of something that is

---

* A reference to Otto Von Ranke's argument that history "should be written the way it really was."—editor's note

really there."[196] What the pluralists laid hold of was the one-party nature of American politics.

In 1956, Daniel Bell wrote that "ideological" movements had repeatedly failed in the politics of pragmatism and that "moral indignation" had played a small role "in the political arena."[197] Five years before, Cecelia Kenyon had said much the same thing about the politics of the Revolutionary era. Defining Paine as outside of realistic politics, she had noted that, "Indeed, for a revolutionary age, the length of the political spectrum from Right to Left was amazingly short."[198]

It is my impression that Bell and Kenyon are correct in their description. Certainly in the early period, I am more impressed with the agreement between such men as Jefferson and John Adams than with the differences between them.[199] One might even take a stab at a general consensus interpretation of Jeffersonians and Federalists: both agreed that gentlemen should rule.[200] Pluralist historians working on other periods have done a successful job of establishing consensus as the central theme *in the political arena*, to use Bell's phrase.

But the fundamental error of the pluralists was a too easy identification of the political arena with the whole society. Bell's definition of "democratic politics" as involving "bargaining between legitimate groups" gives the game away. For who is to decide what is a legitimate group? In practice, it is those with power. Thus from the very beginning, certain groups have been defined as not qualified for full participation in American politics—especially women, poor people, and nonwhite people. Our politics has been a politics of exclusion. In a sense Bell is an authentic Jeffersonian: both are more elitist than democrat.

The pluralist writing history revels in the freedom from conflict, the absence of real issues in American politics. The obverse of this is a more realistic definition of those politics as essentially one-party. The "pragmatic," "non-ideological" party of the legitimate elites has ruled: call it Democratic, call it Republican, through much of our history (with certain notable exceptions) it makes, as the pluralists have shown—with reams of documentation—little difference.[201]

What has been the cost of a politics of exclusion? Our politics have been unreal, purchasing placidity by avoiding real issues, real suffering. By the pluralists' own description, the central theme of the American political tradition has been vacuousness. Thus, for many years, earlier in this century, there was a consensus within national politics concerning black people: there was no problem. The din of congressional consensus masked the anguish and suffering of millions. The bipartisan foreign policy of the post-war years made another political consensus, and when it came to Vietnam, alternatives were defined not in terms of what sane men and women dwelling in the real world proposed, but in terms that made sense only to the people who inhabit the insulated world of our politics.

Thus, viewed realistically, in order to find two parties in America, we must define the "pragmatists"—who, of course, have their ideology, too—as one, and the "ideologues" as the other. But the latter have been barred from politics as "illegitimate," and the pluralists' is only the latest of many attempts to justify that exclusion.

VI. The Ideology of Repression at the End of the 'Sixties

In the late 'sixties, the repression came down again: after a few years of relative tolerance of the New Left, American elites moved once again back to normalcy—back to intolerance and repression. The ideology of the 'fifties was still very much around, often expounded by the same people. Social scientist Daniel Bell was predicting and planning for a year 2000 when, since the only remaining problems are technical rather than political, social science will replace politics as the way of dealing with those remaining nonideological problems.[202] "It's an idea whose time is coming," said Daniel P. Moynihan. Michael Harrington called it "one of the most radical suggestions put forth by a responsible body in our recent history."[203] Meanwhile, Harrington revived another aspect of the anti-democratic faith by pinning the war in Vietnam on what he called "a populistic President."[204] And something called the International Association for Cultural Freedom, "a Paris-based alliance of liberals that seeks to advance the cause of thought," was bringing together, for that purpose, McGeorge Bundy, Kenneth Galbraith, Arthur Schlesinger, Jr., George Kennan, Daniel Bell, Richard Hofstadter, Edward Shils, and C. Vann Woodward.[205]

Eric Hoffer, transmuted into the official philosopher and workingman's representative on presidential commissions, held forth on the racial situation, shouting, "Rage is cheap. Rage is easy. Rage is a luxury. What is really needed is for Negroes to trust each other, to help each other."[206] And, pounding his fist, the philosopher shouted his views on student activism: "we need more chancellors who delight in battle, . . . who love a fight, who get up in the morning and say: 'Who shall I kill today?' "[207] "It would have been a wonderful thing," said Hoffer concerning Columbia, "if Grayson Kirk got mad and got a gun and killed a few."[208]

It is on campus, where the professors are, that the ideology of the 'fifties emerged most clearly in the late 'sixties as the ideology of repression.[209] In the fall of 1967, an orientation program at the University of Wisconsin recommended that incoming freshmen read *The True Believer*. Psychiatrist Bruno Bettelheim described student activists as true believers, "very, very sick," "paranoiacs," trying to resolve the oedipal conflict, "having"—like Unger's historian-rebels —"to beat down father to show they are a big boy."[210] John Roche saw psychiatric roots, too: the radicals were "alienated students" who "want to be loved."[211] While at Berkeley, Lewis Feuer described the student movement in this way:

> The conglomeration [of students] acts as a magnet for the morally corrupt; intellectual lumpen-proletarians, lumpen-beatniks, and lumpen-agitators wend their ways to the university campus to advocate a melange of narcotics, social-perversion, collegiate Castroism and campus Maoism.[212]

Four years later, expatriated to Toronto, Feuer could not get the horrors of Berkeley out of his mind, so he wrote a book, explaining it all in terms of generational conflict; generalizing from his own experience, he attributed many of the disasters of the modern world to student radicals.[213]

In these interpretations the activists are called Nazis or "storm troopers" as often as they are called Communists.[214] Nathan Glazer compared the success of the Free Speech Movement at Berkeley to the success of Lee Harvey Oswald. Before ascending to Harvard, Seymour Martin Lipset, another veteran of the troubles at Berkeley, likened the Free Speech Movement to the KKK and the White Citizens' Councils. Lipset saw another familiar pluralist theme: manipulation of the majority by "a few extremists."[215] In a somewhat antic press conference during the 1969 University of Chicago sit-in, a Nobel Prize-winning cancer researcher saw clear evidence of outside agitation and international Communist conspiracy.[216] And Franklin

L. Ford of Harvard suggested the conspiratorial nature of the 1969 Harvard sit-in with evidence which almost precisely duplicates that which had been offered two centuries before to explain the Boston Tea Party: the demonstrators arrived with chains, crowbars, and "a large supply of miscellaneous keys."[217]

In other words, the pluralists simply applied their model to their own turf. Stability and equilibrium were the goals of society, and since the society called itself democratic, then stability and equilibrium must *be* democracy. Student activism, like other mass movements as seen by the pluralists, "threatens the foundations of democratic order," said Lipset.[218] What Glazer called the "anti-institutional bias"[219] of the New Left was disruptive, anti-democratic, and those who disrupt the equilibrium, whether within the university or in the larger society, must be evil, sick, outside agitators. Stern measures would be necessary to deal with what Jacques Barzun of Columbia called "student despotism."[220]

And so the repression came down, on students and faculty alike, and once again liberals justified it in the name of freedom. In April of 1969 the American Civil Liberties Union sent to 350 colleges and universities a statement which drew the line, in the name of academic freedom, between permissible and impermissible dissent on campus.[221] Immediately the document became a loyalty test in the hands of university officials interviewing prospective faculty.[222] Once again, as so many times before, liberals were initiating and legitimizing repression.

Similar statements came from the American Association of University Professors.[223] In its doctrine and conduct the AAUP has been limited and sometimes directly repressive. The organization's stand on "extramural utterances" holds the faculty member to narrower standards than those existing for the non-academic. When the faculty member "speaks or writes as a citizen," his "social position in the community imposes special obligations." Thus the AAUP condones, under undefined "extraordinary circumstances," "the disciplining of a faculty member for exercising the rights of free speech guaranteed to him as a citizen by the Constitution of the United States. . . ." According to the AAUP, a faculty member violates the "standard of academic responsibility" by "incitement of misconduct, or conceivably some other impropriety of circumstance."[224] In other words, by the AAUP's standards, a faculty member who, to take one instance, supports non-violent but illegal civil disobedience is probably guilty of "unprofessional conduct."

In addition, a recent statement by an administrator that academic freedom in a sense begins with tenure[225] is in accord with the spirit of AAUP doctrine. The AAUP states that it "does not ordinarily exercise jurisdiction" when "institutions or individuals decide that a non-tenure relationship is not to be renewed at the conclusion of a contract period."[226] And in practice the AAUP deals only with abuses against *faculty* of the institution in question, refusing to extend its jurisdiction to those *not hired*. These two refusals eliminate from the AAUP's jurisdiction the vast majority of the current cases. In short, AAUP doctrine protects the powerful and legitimizes the abuse of the powerless.

When I told the Associate Secretary of the AAUP that I had been dismissed in part because of participation in a sit-in in 1966, he riposted, "was it disruptive?"[227] Staughton Lynd was rejected for an appointment at Roosevelt University for what its president called "ad hominem" reasons: Lynd, the president explained, was "publicity prone," a photograph of him carrying a picket sign had appeared in a newspaper, he had been spoken of unfavourably in *Harper's* and in a Chicago newspaper column and was quoted as making statements unacceptable to the administration. The AAUP found no *prima facie* case of a violation of academic freedom to justify investigating the matter, and left it at that.[228]

If the National AAUP often legitimizes repression, local chapters and officials have been known to play leading roles in initiating and cooperating with repression. One historian who participated in a peaceful demonstration on the sidelines during a ROTC parade, was fired summarily and ordered to hand over student records by noon the following day; his class was taken over by the acting president of the campus AAUP.[229] When it was revealed that the University of Chicago was applying political tests to prospective freshmen, the former head of the local AAUP co-authored a document justifying the practice.[230] Some of my own instruction in the value of working within institutions came from participation in an attempt to run a partial slate of candidates for office in the University of Chicago chapter of the AAUP. Confronted with the first dissent seen within the organization in years, the chairman moved the voting ahead of its announced place on the agenda, cut it off abruptly in the middle when more members entered the room, and acted so intemperately that the distinguished professor who we had nominated for president left the room in disgust.

In the late 'sixties, just as a decade before, academic freedom meant the freedom of universities to do the firing themselves, without outside intervention. Thus, the *New York Times* urged government to keep its hands off: "the need now is clearly to permit the colleges to put their own house in order. . . . For Congress to act now would be to endanger both the pacification and the freedom of the American campus."[231] Andrew Cordier, pacifier at Columbia, told a Senate Subcommittee that "stability" on campus would be best achieved not through federal legislation, but "with the instrumentalities and procedures which the university itself must create or now has now at hand.''[232] One of those instrumentalities, it developed, was the device of responding to the McClellan committee's subpoenas of names of activist students (and faculty advisers) by sending only SDS names. University lawyers somehow found the strength to negotiate to withhold the names of moderate students, but as Cordier read the law, he had no choice but to hand over the SDS names.[233]

The same kind of double-think was evident far and wide as crusaders for repression marched under the banners of "academic freedom." During the summer of 1969 hundreds of administrators showed the obverse of the banner, waving their plans for pacification in various offices of the Nixon administration. "There was a parade of these guys coming in all summer about various matters, and naturally the talk got around to campus unrest," said one of the *New York Times'* "informed sources."[234] The *Times* commended the AAUP for speaking out against disruptive students but urged the organization to spell out its implied condemnation of faculty members who condone or participate in such activities.[235] Congressional liberals claimed to be standing up to reaction when they held hearings which justified liberal repression.[236] Hans Morgenthau wrote in the *New Republic* that "law and order" means "violence in defence of the *status quo*," while joining with Edward Shils and others at the University of Chicago to oppose a "coercive" demonstration against the manufacturer of napalm.[237] And the youth of the nation was offered an extended statement of "a moral, ethical or philosophical point of view about dissent and how it may properly—and effectively—be expressed" by Supreme Court Justice Abe Fortas.[238]

On campus, spies were at work: some "students" were narcs, others were taking notes for the FBI, for HUAC, for the local red squad, for the *Chicago Tribune*.[239] Universities went into the same business: at first they were content with still photographs, later they went into movies.[240] Information gathered by student spies for the FBI went to university administrators.[241] Faculty members discovered that if they made the mistake of learning their students' names, they might be called up to name them for disciplinary purposes and put in jeopardy if they were unwilling to do so.[242] On the other hand, many were willing to serve as finger-men.[243] Admissions officers began to devote more attention to the hair-length and politics of candidates for admission, and, as we shall see, eminent faculty utilized the ideology of the 'fifties to justify this attention.

And there was, indeed, violence on the campuses. Less than a week after Hoffer's exhortation to chancellors and mayors to wake up with murder on their minds, James Rector *was* murdered in Berkeley.[244] A few days before, the attempt to murder and mutilate University of Chicago Sociology Professor Richard Flacks occurred.[245] End of ideology showed a starkly barbaric face in the responses of university people. While the radical lay bleeding and paralyzed with a crushed skull and a nearly severed right hand, a university official told the press of the latter wound, but not the former, and suggested that it was suicide. Some senior sociologists also saw it as a suicide attempt and publicly speculated about "what drove him to it."[246] The event caused the department to delay the announcement that Flacks was not being given tenure; they let the word out after the last issue of the student newspaper had been published.*

---

* Professor Flacks was given tenure in the undergraduate college system at the University of Chicago but was denied tenure within the Sociology Department. In this instance, the clear outcome of the two-tiered system was to deny scholarly legitimacy to a noted sociologist. —editors note

So Flacks left the University of Chicago, together with Marlene Dixon.* Staughton Lynd was never allowed in. The same university had expelled forty-three students and suspended eighty-one in 1969.[247] The same thing was happening across the country. Faculty members were being fired[248] and students were being expelled: in the 1968-1969 academic year on twenty-eight campuses over nine hundred students were expelled or suspended for political offenses and more than eight hundred fifty were put on probation.[249]

VII. Historians as Activists, II

Historians, too, have been campus activists. At the University of Chicago, William McNeill urged what he called a "counter revolutionary" policy in regard to the 1969 sit-in.[250] Arthur Mann was a member of the University of Chicago disciplinary committee which handed down the 1969 expulsions, basing its sentences on students' political beliefs rather than their conduct.[251] At Harvard in the spring of 1969, while some students were thinking of ways to abolish ROTC, Oscar Handlin was deeply involved in organizing faculty on the other side. Together with Bernard Bailyn, he presented a proposal whose effect would have been to legitimize a more academically respectable ROTC while at the same time de-legitimizing student-run and student-initiated courses.[252] After the bust, Professor Schlesinger of CUNY wrote that while "invoking the police may on occasion be necessary to preserve academic free-

---

* Marlene Dixon is a left sociologist, then at the University of Chicago. Her firing precipitated a sit-in in January of 1969 "skillfully" and repressively quelled by University President Edward Levy, now Gerald Ford's choice for U.S. Attorney General. Dixon has more recently been involved in Quebec politics and political turmoil at McGill. —editor's note

dom," it had been wrong at Harvard. Not precisely wrong, but rather, imprudent; it was not the fact of "cops clubbing Harvard and Radcliffe students" that offended him but the "spectacle" of it, which "obliged the S.D.S. and illustrated its favorite thesis of the hidden violence of American society." The "sadness of the recent trouble at Harvard" was not that president Nathan Pusey had called the police, but that he had done so before consulting with moderate students and faculty.[253]

Meanwhile, apparently finding the AAUP insufficiently militant in defense of academic freedom, such historians as Oscar Handlin, Daniel Boorstin, Dumas Malone, Marvin Meyers, Louis Gottschalk and Leonard Levy were joining Sidney Hook's "University Centers for Rational Alternatives." (Other members of the new organization included Bruno Bettelheim, Nathan Glazer, David Truman, Edward Teller, S.I. Hayakawa, Lewis Feuer, Leo Strauss, and John Roche.) The UCRA attacked the "extremist putschism" and "extremist terrorism" of the "McCarthyism of the Left," and sought "to promote the activism of non-extremists"; specifically, that activism aimed to oppose "appeasement" and to strengthen the "backbone" of university administrators by justifying the calling in of police to protect academic freedom. UCRA described itself as "non-political" and was tax-exempt.[254]

At Columbia in the violent spring of 1968, Richard Hofstadter was a leader of the pro-administration forces, volunteering his services to Grayson Kirk and working with David Truman to round up faculty support for the tottering administration. In June, Hofstadter was Kirk's choice to deliver the commencement address in his place. There, after the bloody police charges called down upon the university by Kirk and Truman earlier in the spring, Hofstadter spoke of the university's neutrality and its commitment to "certain basic values of freedom, rationality, inquiry, discussion, and to its own internal order. . . ." Endorsing reform, he urged that future plans be based on "an evolution from existing structures and arrangements, not upon a utopian scheme for a perfect university." A year later almost one thousand Columbia faculty members, organized by Hofstadter, Fritz Stern, Jacques Barzun and others paid for an advertisement in the *New York Times* called "The University as a Sanctuary of Academic Freedom." In what President Andrew Cordier called a "statesman-like declaration," the signers reiterated the doctrine of self-regulation: "the university must put its own house in order. . . . Ill-considered intervention by outside forces may only jeopardize academic freedom." Together with the historians named above, and with Daniel Bell and Lionel Trilling, John A. Garraty, Henry Graff, Virginia D. Harrington, William E. Leuchtenburg, Chilton Williamson and other historians insisted that "the tradition of the university as a sanctuary of academic freedom and centre of informed discussion is an honored one, to be guarded vigilantly. . . . It is our intention not to surrender the safeguards of freedom that men have erected at great sacrifice over several centuries." But when Columbia surrendered the names of SDS members to the Senator John McClellan's Subcommittee on investigations, these scholars did not feel called upon to release statesmanlike declarations about the university as a sanctuary of academic freedom.[256]

In the spring of 1967, a young University of Chicago historian, not himself a radical, was shocked by what he found while assisting in admissions work. One folder contained a description of an interview by the Director of Admissions. The interviewer described the candidate as "fingering his long tresses." The student said that he came from a Left family, and that his father had lost his job during the McCarthy period. In his report on this, the interviewer commented, "you can see what kind of a family he comes from." When the student acknowledged that he was an activist, the interviewer commented, "We have enough kids here who cause trouble. Better let him go to Reed or Berkeley." The historian let his indignation get the better of his sense of professionalism—and let the word out. Shortly, he was in serious difficulties for his indiscretion. Those difficulties were caused in part by a statement written by five faculty members, including Daniel Boorstin and a former president of the campus AAUP. What is of interest to us here is not so much the difficulties of the young faculty member as the response of Professors Boorstin *et al.*, for it illustrates quite starkly how it was that the ideology of the 'fifties was, once again in the 'sixties, the ideology of repression. While the President of the University stated that Chicago did not exclude students for political views, the Boorstin statement made it quite clear that such exclusion would be legitimate:

> Within the fremework of the law and in cognizance of the general value consensus [which Boorstin saw as] prevailing in our society, it is the right of the University faculty and administrative officers to determine what shall be the orientation, social mission, intellectual culture, curriculum, and educational goals of the University.

It was, the document concluded, the right of the university "to determine how the pursuit of these goals is to be perpetuated through the choice of the succeeding generation of scholars."[257]

What Boorstin had offered was consensus ideology in its most nakedly exclusionist form. (Subsequently, a university committee built on Boorstin's doctrine when it defined the crime of "treason" against the university.)[258] Assuming consensus in the society, and taking it upon himself to define the content of that consensus, Boorstin saw it as right and good that those who did not adhere to the consensus be excluded from the university. Boorstin's "general value consensus" was also used to justify the exclusion of faculty who did not partake of the consensus. Writing for the Associated Press in more than one hundred newspapers across the country on "Good-By, Mr. Chips: The Dissenting Professors," Boorstin noted that, more and more, we were hearing of professors who support the Vietcong, professors who are not opposed to premarital intercourse, professors who announce other "unpopular or outlandish" views.[259] Why were these people going against the consensus? In part, not out of antagonism to the community but out of involvement with it as the profession grew and diversified and professors had more to say about more things. Boorstin looked with approval at the rapprochement between business and the academy, mentioning a university chancellor who resigned to become a vice president of Standard Oil, and the resignation of the president of the American Stock Exchange to become president of Wesleyan University. But there was a negative side to the dissent of the professors, and this was Boorstin's focus. They were out to advance themselves, said Boorstin, and "publicity builds academic careers. . . ." (He cited such noted dissenters as Daniel P. Moynihan.) Dissent was idiosyncratic and it was no assurance of "vigor or independence of mind." Claiming to favour *true* dissent, Boorstin worried about the bad effects of what he imagined to be the dissenters' "academic immunity." "Reputable institutions," he wrote, have been overtolerant of dissenters, "doubly cautious lest they underestimate the professional competence of dissenters, not infrequently they lean over backward to avoid the shadow of intolerance." And what if the dissenting professor should be fired? That was no cause for concern: "he is almost certain to become somebody's hero."

This piece brings us full circle, back to Boorstin's Quakers three centuries before. They are simply modern dissenters in old-style dress. Boorstin shows as much concern for the professors' freedom as he did for the Quakers'. In each instance, the dissenter is a threat to social stability, and we must not allow tolerance to endanger that stability.

In a 1969 commencement address, true to his reading of past radical movements, Boorstin saw contemporary student radicals as "reactionaries," "dyspeptics and psychotics." Students, whether black or white, did not know how well off they were: "about 40 per cent of the students are women," and "even ten years ago, there were more Negroes attending American colleges and universities than the total college population of England or of France." This sham comparison was followed by other versions of "you never had it so good." If American students thought their housing and social facilities inadequate, let them "take a quick trip to Paris [the Sorbonne], where there are no social facilities at all." Not enough democracy in the American university? "Let . . . them read the sign, yellowed with age, at the entrance to the Sorbonne, warning that to use these premises for political discussions is illegal." Speaking especially of black admission demands, Boorstin reminded his audience that "In the university all men are *not* equal." He endorsed Jefferson's "natural aristocracy." Those faculty members who believed in "the mission of their universities" must not become "Professor Toms," must not surrender to the growing tendency to "Spiritual Appeasement." "The university must be a place of respect for and preference for intellectual superiority": "every other kind of non-intellectual exceptionalism," whether white racism or "Black Brahminism," was "a cancer."[260]

The term "cancer" ties together Boorstin's views of dissent in the past and in the present, on campus and off. Speaking on Vietnam, Boorstin told a convention of Associated Press Managing Editors, "It seems to me that dissent is the great problem of America today."[261] "Disagreements"—such as declarations by organized homosexuals—were "good", but dissent led to "dissension," "discord"; if "disagreement" was "the life blood of democracy," dissension was its "cancer."[262] Choosing the "sniper's bullet" as "an eloquent expression of dissent," Boorstin described dissenters in the familiar idiosyncratic terms: the dissenter sought personal power, dissenting for dissent's sake, setting up magazines which do nothing but dissent.[263] The dissenters' "main object" was "to preserve and conceal their separate identity as a dissenting minority." Here lay the heart of Boorstin's general theory, a totalitarian ideology dedicated to the destruction of anything that hinted at differentness. If the unwillingness of "the dissenting pack" to compromise was a threat to society, so was the immigrant's assertion of a right "to remain different." The very "affirmation of differentness," whether the dissenter's, the immigrant's, or the black student's would tend to destroy our institutions. That is the ideology which Boorstin uses to justify contemporary repression, and it is only a somewhat more extreme form of the ideology which his "politically neutral" colleagues imposed on the American past.

The number of historians who, like Boorstin, have become off-campus activists, is legion, and space does not allow a full description of their activities here. A sampling might include urban historian Richard Wade, campaigner for various Kennedys and for Mayor Daley. Wade told a 1968 American Historical Association meeting that it is improper for academics to identify their institutions with their individual political activities;[264] he neglected to recall that he had allowed not only his name but also a photograph of himself teaching a University of Chicago class to appear as part of

"Faculty for Daley's" campaign literature.[265] As we shall see, this very partisan activism had its effect on Wade's reading of the American past.[266] (In the present, it led to appointment by Daley as a Commissioner of the Chicago Housing Authority.)

At the end of 1967, after the teach-ins and with rising anti-war feeling on the campuses, Oscar Handlin felt that it was time for the "moderate segment of the academic community" to be heard. Handlin and a small group of activists sponsored by Freedom House* urged that the United States "stay the course with a limited war. . . ." Specifically, they endorsed a strategy of "seize and hold" rather than "search and destroy"; there must be no "abandonment of our commitments." The tide of "isolationist" sentiment had to be stopped, and those who criticized Johnson's policy must be aware that they were contributing as much, in their way, to the war's outcome as were the troops in Vietnam. It was time to "desist from the excessive spirit of *mea culpa* which permeates certain quarters of American society." "We can be justly proud of our international accomplishments during the past twenty years."[267]

Handlin and his colleagues justified American Vietnam policy in the context of a kind of international pluralism. They accepted unquestioningly the goal of "political equilibrium" as if equilibrium were democracy and there were no *victims* of that equilibrium. And, true to pluralist dogma, disequilibrium had its orgins in "externally directed subversion." "For the foreseeable future," said the document, "the American nuclear umbrella will be a vital element in any over-all Asian equilibrium." Such statements lend strong support to C. Wright Mills' contention that end

---

* A New York City organization with a strongly anti-communist social democratic flavour. —editor's note

of ideology was simply "a consensus of a few provincials about their own immediate and provincial position." And, as we shall see, Handlin's activism, too, translated very directly into the history which he wrote.[268]

The activism of Arthur M. Schlesinger, Jr., of course provides the example most envied by historians, the standard against which thousands of competitors must measure themselves. As Gordon Craig has put it, it is the intellectuals who, "after all, create the Camelots of this world,"[269] and Schlesinger, who rejoiced in the title, "court philosopher,"[270] did his part. He put history at the service of power, rewriting the history of the Cuban Revolution in order to legitimize, in advance, the Bay of Pigs.[271] "Defeated by the moral issue," he had helped to keep the invasion story out of the press.[272] Unable to find the internal resources to "blow the whistle" on the Bay of Pigs in 1961,[273] in 1966 he decisively proclaimed, "surely the time has come to blow the whistle before the present burst of revisionism regarding the origins of the cold war goes much further."[274] Later, he acknowledged that the last remark was "intemperate";[275] he has yet to say the same for the rest of his conduct. And in December of 1968 the assembled members of the American Historical Association remained silent while Schlesinger lectured them on the need for "civility."[276]

In the late 'sixties, Schlesinger again agitated for a strong executive, as he had a decade before. But by this time Vietnam had brought home to him a possibility which he had earlier ignored: presidential power might have its "excesses." So he devised a new scheme, which repeated his earlier errors, but in new form: the president had too much power in foreign affairs, but not enough in the domestic realm. Thus, in a time of increasing repression, Schlesinger opened the way to more, with such fictitious distinctions as the claim that while acts in foreign policy were generally irreversible, domestic acts were generally reversible. After all, he said—with amazing blindness in a time of internal convulsion—the president "represents the whole people, and the answer to the crisis of alienation surely does not lie in the weakening of the centre. . . ."[277]

Schlesinger does indeed write as he votes and vote as he writes, and it is hard to find a line of demarcation between his politics and his scholarship. But we have seen that, although he has risen to greater eminence than most, Schlesinger is but the archetype of his generation, a generation of activists. This activism is amply reflected in the historical associations and in their journals. It is there in a review which endorses uncritically a book on chemical warfare written "from the policy standpoint" and without "emotionalism."[278] It is there in articles and reviews which attack Left scholarship with an acerbity unmatched by anyone on the Left. Oscar Handlin set the style in 1962, when he characterized William Appleman Williams' *Contours of American History* as "an elaborate hoax," "uproariously funny," "farcical," a "total diaster," "altogether incoherent."[279] John Higham described the review as "tasteless and irresponsible," "a scandalously intemperate polemic,"[280] and much the same might be said of some of the reviews of Barton J. Bernstein's *Towards a New Past*. Charles Mullett called the writers "arrogant" and "selfrighteous" while characterizing my essay on the American Revolution "from the bottom up" as an attempt "to get at the feelings of dirty people with no names," including merchant seamen, "scarcely to be regarded as an important sector of society."[281] John Garraty of Columbia dealt with my work by remarking, inscrutably, that I "represent the New Left's Left."[282] David Donald delivered himself of a similarly genteel polemic,[283] and Irwin Unger found his "blood pressure" rising as he reviewed the book.[284] Finally, a Columbia activist even found a review of a book about fourteenth-century Europe an appropriate place for an attack on the "intolerable self-righteousness" of the New Left.[285]

Organizationally, we find the American Historical Association conducting itself in accord with pluralist practice: when it appeared that the membership might, for the first time in years, attempt actively to involve itself in the affairs of the organization, the Council proposed to change the constitution with measures which would centralize power in the Council and lessen the possibility for meaningful debate by doing away with the last institution within the organization which even remotely resembled a town meeting. All of this was done, with traditional pluralist irony, in the name of making the organization more responsive to "the will of the membership."[286]

In the 'sixties, presidential addresses of the AHA and the Organization of American Historians remained activist and political, and, as in the past, reflected a very narrow range of politics and activism. Samuel Flagg Bemis' "American Foreign Policy and the Blessings of Liberty"[287] and John K. Fairbank's "Assignment for the 'Seventies"[288] continued to wage Cold War, the former more ostentatiously than the latter, but both in agreement in opposing revolutions and in denying the possibility of an American imperialism. Fairbank was ethnocentric and condescending in his approach to "our China problem." Aggression came from China, not from the United States. The war in Vietnam was a "disaster," but "inadvertent," brought about by "an excess of righteousness and disinterested benevolence." It was *our* "crown of thorns"—not Vietnam's.[289]

In his "Mythmakers of American History," Thomas Bailey told the OAH that the "Robber Barons" were instead industrial statesmen, and the Cold-War revisionists were "the self-flagellation school," He incited to riot with the following words from another era: "The luckless African-

Americans while in slavery were essentially in jail; and we would certainly not write the story of a nation in terms of its prison population." All of these remarks were presented as coming forth from one who was himself above the battle, one who could fret over "presentitis" and condemn historians for being "hysterians." "Sometimes," the noted diplomatic historian remarked, "historians degenerate into polemicists."[290]

Finally, to return at the end to history itself, let us note a few examples of the history produced in the late 'sixties by non-Left historians. Here is Richard Wade, in the course of a discussion of nineteenth century New York reformer Jacob Riis, surrendering his critical sense in the face of Mayor Daley's prediction of an imminent end to slums.[291] Daley, Wade tells us, belongs right up there among the great men of Illinois, along with Abraham Lincoln and Adlai Stevenson.[292] Here is Henry Steele Commager, contrasting the "creative and constructive character" of the revolution of 1776 with the "negative and destructive character" of today's "revolutionary fervor." Those who made the first Revolution "broke up an Empire, to be sure," but

> What is more important is what they put in the place of that which they overthrew or destroyed. They were not blinded by hostility to the old system, or by personal enmity toward the Establishment; they knew what they were about; they had a program, and they carried it out, item by item, to a triumphant conclusion.

They even "worked through political channels for realizable ends. . . ." All this is in sharp contrast with today's revolutionaries who are without a program and idiosyncratic in motivation.[293]

This sort of political harangue is making its way into the textbooks. Thus Oscar Handlin has translated Freedom House doctrine on Vietnam directly into his *History of the*

United States.[294] Handlin, a "Professor for Humphrey,"[295] uncritically defends American policy in Vietnam —where Ho Chi Minh was "reckless about the cost in lives" —and places that defense in the context of an overall justification of recent American foreign policy:

> For more than a decade, *disruptive* new forces touched off a succession of incidents that kept the world on the verge of war. Latin America, Asia and Africa seethed with unrest. In those vast areas, nationalism and social revolution kept *disturbing existing conditions* and readily spread across *established boundary lines*. Through the difficult years after 1960, the United States pursued a tortuous course, struggling to avoid war yet determined to honor its commitments to freedom.[296]

The unasked question here, as in other pluralist analyses, is, just what is disruptive? The rebellion of the Latin American, Asian, and African, or the conditions of their daily lives? Why are existing conditions and established boundary lines thought of as good? Is rebellion disruptive, or the conditions which lead to it?

In conclusion, for a glimpse of a synthesis of America in the 'sixties as seen through the lens of consensus, we may turn to the sixth edition of Morison and Commager's *Growth of the American Republic*.[297] The last chapter, written by Columbia faculty activist William E. Leuchtenburg,[298] is entitled "The Great Society at War." On Vietnam, he is critical of Johnson, but critical because the President's policy was not "prudent." "Month by month," writes Leuchtenburg, "the war reeled farther out of control." It was not as if anyone was making bad decisions; apparently, just as Niebuhr and Schlesinger had argued many years before, things, not people, were in control. Nonetheless, the war was finally slowed by an anti-war movement. Where did this movement originate? Apparently it started in the U.S.

Senate in 1965, where "hawks" were opposed to "doves."[299] Senators Wayne Morse and Ernest Gruening were "doves"; later they were joined by other senators, mainly Democrats. Leuchtenburg gives much attention to the attitudes and activities of the war's "critics," "opponents," "doves." Who were they? The only people named are some U.S. Senators, Richard Goodwin, Harrison Salisbury, David M. Shoup, and James Reston.*[300] Some of us remember it differently. Some of us remember that there was, to begin with, an extra-parliamentary anti-war movement which expended enormous energy in the attempt to force the real issues into the vacuous bipartisan politics of the day. Some of us remember that William Fulbright voted for the Tonkin Bay Resolution when others knew better. Some of us remember the courage with which Robert Kennedy invested his charisma in the anti-war movement, oh so early, so alone. Some of us remember marches on Washington, the Assembly of Unrepresented People, the International Days of Protest, sit-ins, arrests, firings.[301] But either our memory is false, or this is really 1984. For Leuchtenburg, the first and only partial mention of such extra-institutional struggles comes *after* a description of the doves against the hawks. *After* "the administration ignored the counsel of opponents of its Vietnam policy, its critics escalated their activities too, from 'teach-ins' on campuses and demonstrations at which draft cards were burned to more violent confrontations with authority."[302] At first it was doves against hawks, with responsible men leading the peace movement, and *then* the irresponsibles took over.

If the responsibles have Leuchtenburg's blessing, the irresponsibles do not. Anti-war leaders began to insist that

---

* Richard Goodwin is a former John F. Kennedy aide; Salsibury and Reston are both of the *New York Times*; Shoup was former commander of the Marine Corp. —editor's note

what Leuchtenburg calls "riots" were legitimate. John Gardner is quoted on "the rage to demolish." And there were other riots. The assassination of Martin Luther King set off "race riots" across the country. "Race riots": that is what Leuchtenburg calls it when the army, the national guard, and the police are at war with black people. But the army, the national guard, the police play a very small role in Leuchtenburg's history. He tells us that "the residents of Resurrection City were routed with tear gas, and the camp was demolished." Who did this? Leuchtenburg's passive voice leaves us with a vision of tear gas falling from the sky like rain; once again, *things* were in control, not men.[303]

Thus violence was on the upsurge in America: there were assassinations and bombings, a rising crime rate, slaughter on television, "coercion by students at Columbia and other universities," and "lobbying by the National Rifle Association against effective gun control legislation."[304] Again, there is the equation of Left and Right, the politics which says that there is really no difference between a college sit-in and the bombing of a Birmingham church.

In 1968 Senator Eugene McCarthy's "Children's Crusade" "demonstrated that the political process was remarkably responsive to the popular will." But to Chicago there also came "itinerant revolutionists bent on provoking a violent confrontation." Their visit seems wholly irrational, since says Leuchtenburg, "In most respects the convention was exceptionally democratic. . . ." Of course, some of the followers of McCarthy, McGovern, and Kennedy "believed" that "the will of the people had been flouted" when Humphrey was nominated, but in Leuchtenburg's book, that is only a "belief." Meanwhile, out in the streets, this "exceptionally democratic" convention was being "marred" by demonstrators, "a number of whom were deliberately provocative." Some of Daley's police used their clubs "indiscriminately." Like the war in Vietnam, they were "out of control."[305]

* * * * *

Leuchtenburg's students just don't believe him any more. Nor do they believe Professors Commager, Nevins, Boorstin, Schlesinger, Handlin, or Morison. It is the Left which has spoken to them of real issues, of pain and suffering, and of a better world which has *not* been seen before. The politics which mainstream historians have admired are unreal and unprincipled; their history has aimed further to insulate those politics from reality. But the Left will continue to present the real alternatives, the alternatives which expose the triviality of America's politics of pragmatism. Fire us, expel us, jail us, we will not go away. We exist, and people like us have existed throughout history, and we will simply not allow you the luxury of continuing to call yourselves politically neutral while you exclude all of this from your history. You cannot lecture us on civility while you legitimize barbarity. You cannot fire us for activism without having your own activism exposed. You cannot call apologetics "excellence" without expecting the most rigorous and aggressive of scholarly replies.

We were at the Democratic Convention, and at the steps of the Pentagon, and we will not go away. We are even in the Shoreham and the Sheraton Park.* And we are in the libraries, writing history, trying to cure it of your partisan and self-congratulatory fictions, trying to come a little closer to finding out how things actually were.

* Washington hotels which housed the meeting where this paper was first delivered. —editor's note

NOTES

I

1. Merle Curti chaired the session; the other panelists were John Braeman, William Appleman Williams, and Lawrence R. Veysey. Unger's paper was published as "The 'New Left' and American History: Some Recent Trends in United States Historiography," *American Historical Review*, LXXII (July 1967), 1237-1263.

2. *Ibid.*, 1261, 1259, 1244n., 1242, 1249, 1246. See, for instance, Unger's summary of New Left interpretations of American foreign policy: "Free trade, foreign investment, Point Four aid—all, presumably, have been tools of American hegemony" (1248; see also 1249).

3. *Ibid.*, 1249, 1253.

4. *Ibid.*, 1249, 1253, 1252, 1263.

5. *Ibid.*, 1262, 1243.

6. Consider the academic careers—or, more precisely, the lack of academic careers—of such historians as Philip S. Foner and Herbert Aptheker. (It should be noted that Aptheker's appointment as visiting lecturer in the Black Studies programme at Bryn Mawr College in 1969-70 came about as a result of student initiative. Aptheker has told the author that in the twenty-four years preceding he actively sought employment at approximately fifty institutions without success.) For a discussion of academic repression in the period after World War II, see below. For the early 'forties, consider especially the Rapp-Coudert investigations in New York City (1940-41) which led to the firing, suspension, or resignation under pressure of approximately fifty faculty members employed by the Board of Higher Education, including historians Philip S. Foner, Jack Foner, Herbert Morais, and Irving Mark. See Lawrence H. Chamberlain, *Loyalty and Legislative Action: A Survey of Activity by the New York State Legislature, 1919-1949* (Ithaca, 1951), 68-186; Robert W. Iversen, *The Communists and the Schools* (New York, 1959), 208-223. Morris Schappes, who was in the English Department at City College at the time, was convicted of perjury and served thirteen and one half months in jail. (See Louis Lerman, ed., *Morris U. Schappes: Letters from the Tombs* [New York, 1941]. I am indebted to Schappes and to Philip S. Foner for information concerning Rapp-Coudert.)

For an earlier period, consider the circumstances of Charles A. Beard's resignation from Columbia: Richard Hofstadter, *The Progressive Historians: Turner, Beard, Parrington* (New York, 1968), 286-288; *New York Times*, editorial ("Columbia's Deliverance"), October 10, 1917, 10. For the experience of Scott Nearing, a Socialist economist, see Lightner Witmer, *The Nearing Case* (New York, 1915); James Weinstein, *The Corporate Ideal in the Liberal State: 1900-1918* (Boston, 1968), 129, 244.

7. LXXIV (December 1968), 531-533.
8. Due to the departure of Staughton Lynd from Yale and of myself from the University of Chicago.
9. For Lynd's conflicts with Yale and with the other institutions noted below, see his "Academic Freedom: Your Story and Mine," *Columbia University Forum*, X (Fall 1967), 23-28 (cf. Edmund S. Morgan and C. Vann Woodward, "Academic Freedom: Whose Story?," *ibid.*, XI [Spring 1968], 42-43; reply by Lynd, *ibid.*, 50-51); (Jesse Lemisch), "No Work for Lynd" and "Draft Statement of NUC Defence Committee," *New University Conference Newsletter*, May 24 , 1968; *New York Times*, July 18, 1967; *Chicago Illini* (University of Illinois, Chicago), July 31, 1967; *Roosevelt Torch*, April 22, 29, May 6, 13, 1968; Mary O'Connell, "Maguire Vetoes Lynd Hiring," *Loyola News* (Chicago), May 10, 1968; fact sheets of Committee for Academic Freedom in Illinois and correspondence among the Committee, the American Association of University Professors, and Staughton Lynd, 1967-69 (in possession of the author).
10. William Hardy McNeill, in conversation with the author, Chicago, December 16, 1966. For some of the factors in my non-renewal —including both my scholarship and my participation in a 1966 sit-in protesting the sending of class rank to Selective Service —see Jesse Lemisch, "Some Remarks on the Lemisch Case," *Chicago Maroon*, May 19, 1967; *idem*, letter to the editor, *ibid.*, November 3, 1967. For a suggestion of McNeill's own capacity for partisanship, see his *The Greek Dilemma: War and Aftermath* (Philadelphia, 1947). (Cf. review by L.S. Stavrianos, *American Historical Review*, LIII [October 1947], 143-144; Gabriel Kolko, *The Politics of War: The World and United States Foreign Policy, 1943-1945* [New York, 1968].) See also Frank Smothers, William Hardy McNeill, Elizabeth Darbishire McNeill, *Report on the Greeks: Findings of a Twentieth Century Fund Team Which Surveyed Conditions in Greece in 1947* (New York, 1948).

For the convictions and scholarship of Daniel J. Boorstin, Richard

Wade, and Arthur Mann of the History Department at the University of Chicago, see below.

11. Consider, for instance, the political difficulties of Eugene D. Genovese at Rutgers, before his appointment at Rochester, and at other institutions which made preliminary approaches to him but did not follow through with offers of employment. Or consider the fact that when the *Chicago Tribune* carried an account of a paper which Christopher Lasch presented at the Socialist Scholars' Conference in September 1968 on the role of socialist intellectuals, Northwestern University's president saw fit to make inquiries of Lasch's chairman, and the chairman thought it entirely appropriate that he do so: telephone conversation between Richard Leopold and the author, November 5, 1968. (Lasch and Genovese are somewhat special cases in that, despite Unger's label, they do not choose to identify with the New Left and they are in some ways hostile to student activism and in disagreement with the New Left's anti-hierarchalism.)

12. See below.

13. *New York Times*, February 8, 1968, 28; February 9, 1968, 1, 56; February 10, 1968, 23; December 21, 1968.

14. See below.

15. Unger, "New Left," 1263, 1262.

II

16. This is of course a historiographical question of limited importance, since the primary question must be whether the history itself is sound, regardless of the historian's motivations. But the contention is so nearly an article of faith and has been so largely unchallenged—with the exception of some of the items listed in my acknowledgments, above, and a few other instances cited below—that it requires consideration in itself. And such consideration inevitably involves us, to some degree, in an evaluation of the content and validity of the history.

17. For a summary and discussion of works by Gar Alperovitz, David Horowitz, D.F. Fleming, William Appleman Williams, and others, see Christopher Lasch, "The Cold War, Revisited and Revisioned," *New York Times Magazine*, January 14, 1968, 26 ff.; see also Kolko, *Politics of War*, and *idem, The Roots of American Foreign Policy: An Analysis of Power and Purpose* (Boston, 1969).

18. For historians seeking to understand repression in American history, a fruitful approach might start with the conception that perhaps

repression is the *normal* state in this country's history, and that what needs explaining are the *aberrations*, those rare periods of free and diverse expression. For one of many studies which, while not intending to lead to such a generalization, seems to provide data for it, see Leonard W. Levy, *Freedom of Speech and Press in Early American History: Legacy of Suppression* (New York, 1963).

19. John Steinke and James Weinstein, "McCarthy and the Liberals," *Studies on the Left*, II (1962), number 3, 43-50.

20. Carey McWilliams, *Witch Hunt: The Revival of Heresy* (Boston, 1950), 16.

21. See Corliss Lamont, ed., *The Trial of Elizabeth Gurley Flynn by the American Civil Liberties Union* (New York, 1968); Barbara Deming, "The Ordeal of SANE," *The Nation*, March 11, 1961, 200-205; A.J. Muste, "The Crisis in SANE," *Liberation*, July-August, 1960, November, 1960, 5-8; *idem*, "Senator Dodd, Norman Cousins, and SANE," *ibid.*, December 1960, 3-4.

22. See especially Sidney Hook, "The Dangers of Cultural Vigilantism," *New York Times Magazine*, September 30, 1951. The centrality of the theme of "cultural vigilantism" is noted in Lasch, "Cultural Cold War," 338-339.

23. *An End to Innocence: Essays in Culture and Politics* (Boston, 1955), 72.

24. *The Vital Center: The Politics of Freedom* (Boston, 1962 [1st ed., 1949]), 102.

25. Letter to the editor of the *Harvard Crimson*, January 7, 1953 (mimeograph).

26. American Civil Liberties Union, *"We hold these truths . . ." Freedom, Justice, Equality: Report on Civil Liberties, January 1951-June 1953* (New York, 1953), 82. For a discussion of the ACLU's "split personality" on the right to travel, see I.F. Stone, *The Truman Era* (New York, 1953), 103-105. See also John Roche, "We've Never Had More Freedom," *New Republic*, Janaury 23, 30, February 6, 1956. Roche, who was then on the faculty at Haverford College, was also director of the Pennsylvania Branch of the ACLU (Cf. Michael Harrington, "Coué and the Liberals," *Dissent*, III [Spring 1956], 214-215.)

27. *Vital Center*, 129.

28. E. Houston Harsha, "The Broyles Commission" in Walter Gellhorn, ed., *The States and Subversion* (Ithaca, 1952), 99. William P. Rogers, then a Senate investigator and subsequently President Richard Nixon's Secretary of State, had advised Illinois State Senator Paul Broyles, "If there is anything you can do financially to them [universities], that is what hurts." (*Ibid.*, 69).

29. *Harvard Crimson*, June 17, 1952, M-9.
30. *New York Times*, June 22, 1949, 34.
31. This is only a small fraction of the institutions involved. See many footnotes throughout this paper. There is not space here for adequate citation, but a general account can be found in the *Annual Reports* of the ACLU, and in such sources as *Harvard Crimson*, June 17, 1952; *U.S. News & World Report*, July 31, 1953.
32. *Harvard Crimson*, June 17, 1952, M-9; Thomas I. Emerson and David Haber, eds., *Political and Civil Rights in the United States: A Collection of Legal and Related Materials* (Buffalo, 1952), 834-836.
33. *New York Times*, January 26, 1953.
34. *Harvard Crimson*, November 10, 1953.
35. *New York Times*, June 22, 1949, 34; *ibid.*, February 18, 1952.
36. Harsha, "Broyles Commission," 100, 97, 96. Hutchins indicated that he did indeed oppose the employment of those who were "engaged in subversive activities" (103).
37. *New York Times*, March 31, 1953, 1, 12, 13. Perhaps more basic than the issue of the Fifth Amendment was the fact that there is no Fifth Amendment *intramurally*. According to the AAU statement, the professor "owes his colleagues . . . complete candor. . . ." The American Association of University Professors concurred:

> The professor who elects to answer his institution's questions may run the risk of losing the protection of the Fifth Amendment, if he has previously invoked the privilege against self-incrimination in refusing to answer similar questions put to him by a government agency. But this consideration should yield to the institution's interest in knowing the facts. Under these circumstances the institution ought to be willing to accept an offer by the professor to answer privately and off the record, or to recognize that such an offer is in itself some evidence of candor and sincerity on the part of the teacher.

Conversely, the professor not making such an offer "must accept the burden of explaining his refusal." If he were attempting "to conceal derogatory information, his silence may reflect unfavourably upon him." On the other hand, if his refusal were based on "honest adherence to principle," although "his silence should not, in itself, be viewed as discreditable," the professor who "persists in silence" should remember that his silence might leave unchallenged evidence questioning his "professional fitness." See Robert K. Carr, "Academic Freedom, the American Association of University Professors, and the United States Supreme Court," *AAUP Bulletin*, XLV (March 1959), 8-10.
38. *New York Times*, March 31, 1953, 12.
39. For a classic statement of the position that "the enterprise of higher

education is essentially aristocratic," see Howard Mumford Jones, "The American Concept of Academic Freedom," *AAUP Bulletin*, XLVI (March 1960), 70-71.

40. See *New York Times*, March 21, 1958.
41. See accounts of Lloyd Barenblatt, H. Chandler Davis, and Paul Rosenkrantz in Committee of First Amendment Defendants, *Behind Bars for the First Amendment* (New York, [1960]).
42. For the Barenblatt decision, see *New York Times*, June 9, 1959; Ralph F. Fuchs, "The Barenblatt Decision of the Supreme Court and the Academic Profession," *AAUP Bulletin*, XLV (September 1959), 333-338.
43. For the attempt to murder Professor Tom Parkinson which resulted in the death of graduate student Stephen Mann Thomas, see David Wesley, *Hate Groups and the Un-American Activities Committee* (New York, 1962), 3-4.
44. Joseph P. Lyford, "Social Science Teachers and the 'Difficult Years'," *AAUP Bulletin*, XLIII (December 1957), 636-645.
45. See above, note 26.

III

46. *America, Russia, and the Cold War, 1945-1966* (New York, 1967), 40.
47. *The Irony of American History* (New York, 1962 [1st ed., 1952]), 16, 6, 13.
48. 'Quoted in Aptheker, *Laureates*, 86. My account has been influenced by Aptheker's essay on Niebuhr and other "New Conservatives" (*ibid.*, 78-93) and his essay on Schlesinger in *Era of McCarthyism*, 115-129.
49. Niebuhr, *Irony*, 159, 108, 75, 88, 89, 67.
50. *Ibid.*, 89.
51. Schlesinger, *Vital Center*, 240; *idem, The Politics of Hope* (Boston, 1963), 73.
52. *Vital Center*, 40-41.
53. *Ibid.*, 254. For a qualification, see *ibid.*, 55: ". . . most basic problems are insoluble."
54. See, for example, *ibid.*, 10; *Politics of Hope*, 70.
55. *Vital Center*, 10. Power modified Schlesinger's ideology a bit; perhaps he realized that an unqualified pessimism made the politics which became his primary occupation seem pointless. As an adviser to President Kennedy, he looked back at the "forgotten nightmare"

of the Eisenhower era. Rejecting the complaint of the 'fifties- —presumably including his own—"that our capacity for progress is extinct," he complained instead that not enough progress had been made. Still, it would not do to overdo this optimism: even what Schlesinger called "the Party of Hope" had "no belief that mortal men can attain Utopia, no faith that fundamental problems have final solutions" (*Politics of Hope*, xi).

56. *Ibid.*, 47, 125; *Vital Center*, ix. See also the discussion below of Schlesinger's essay on the causes of the Civil War.

57. For example, *Politics of Hope*, 124; *Vital Center*, 147; cf. Niebuhr, *Irony*, ix.

58. *Ibid.*, 17, 29; emphasis added.

59. *Vital Center*, 39.

60. *Ibid.*, xxiii, 7, 39, 57, 40, 165, 45.

61. For some of the experimental work upon which I base my conclusions, see Stanley Milgram's experiments on obedience and authority cited in Jesse Jemisch, "Listening to the 'Inarticulate': William Widger's Dream and the Loyalties of American Revolutionary Seamen in British Prisons," *Journal of Social History*, III (Fall, 1969), note 10. For a discussion of work by Milgram, Stanley Schachter and J.E. Singer, and other psychologists, and the implications of that work for theories of human nature and behaviour, see Naomi Weisstein, "Woman as Nigger," *Psychology Today*, October 1969, 22, 58. (It should be noted that Milgram did not test subjects for political orientation.)

62. Niebuhr, *Irony*, 45, 29, 57.

63. Schlesinger, *Vital Center*, 2, xiv.

64. Reprinted in *idem, Politics of Hope*, 92.

65. Niebuhr, *Irony*, 14, 102, 103.

66. *Ibid.*, 101; see also 31.

67. See *ibid.*, 100.

68. John Kenneth Galbraith, *American Capitalism: The Concept of Countervailing Power* (Boston, 1952).

69. See works by David Truman, Talcott Parsons, Nelson Polsby, Robert Dahl, Daniel Bell, David Riesman, Seymour Martin Lipset, and others.

70. Daniel Bell, "Passion and Politics in America," *Encounter*, VI (January 1956), 61.

71. Those who adhered to the ideology did not, in every case, adopt it in its totality. Niebuhr, for instance, dismissed the idea of managing human affairs through social science as "the speculations of our wise men" (*Irony*, 18; see also 80).

72. Bell, "Passion and Politics," 61, 54.
73. Schlesinger, *Vital Center*, 104.
74. See *New York Times*, May 14, 1968.
75. See numerous CBS television programs in the late 'sixties.
76. For excellent analyses, see Paul Breines and Peter Wiley, *Would You Believe . . . ? An Introductory Critique of The True Believer; and Eric Hoffer and Cold War Ideology* (Madison, Wisconsin [n.d.]).
77. Tocqueville was widely admired, assigned, printed and re-printed, and abundantly quoted. Invoking Tocqueville —or sometimes Henry Adams—was in the 'fifties a way in which liberals could sanctify their own essentially conservative thought without having to identify themselves with Burke; nonetheless, many seemed not to mind such identification (see, for instance, Niebuhr, *Irony*, 89; Schlesinger, *Vital Center*, 240; *idem, Politics of Hope*, 73).
78. Roche, "We've Never Had More Freedom," January 23, 1956, 12.
79. Fiedler, *End to Innocence*, 87, 57, 81, 76.
80. See Clifton Brock, *Americans for Democratic Action: Its Role in National Politics* (Washington, D.C., 1962).
81. See Lasch, "Cultural Cold War." The National Association of Manufacturers also adopted the ideology. "Watch Out for Big Talk!" a comic book published in 1950 by the N.A.M.'s United Business Committee and addressed to workers, warned of the dangers of the radical's "'Big Plan' Malarkey."
82. For unrepentant responses to the CIA revelations, see comments by Daniel Bell, Sidney Hook, Arthur Schlesinger, Jr., and others in "Liberal Anti-Communism Revisited: A Symposium," *Commentary*, September 1967, 31-79 (but cf. the response of Richard Rovere, *ibid*., 67-68). On the question of conspiracy, the later reaction of Irving Kristol, who was editor of *Encounter*, is especially interesting. During his editorship, Kristol later recalled,

> Rumours there were, but they were not particularly credible. Most of these rumours issued from sources —Left-wing, anti-American, or both—that would have been happy to circulate them, true or not, and one discounted them in advance. [Irving Kristol, "Memoirs of a 'Cold Warrior'," *New York Times Magazine*, February 11, 1968, 25.]

In other words, any evidence of conspiracy was false because its source was tainted. This is a suggestion of how the end of ideologists handled evidence.
83. See Rogin, *McCarthy*, 84-103; quotations at 100, 99, 84.
84. *Ibid*., 136-247; see also 261-262 for a general summary of the differences in electoral support between McCarthy and agrarian radicalism. Rogin alludes, of course, to Daniel Bell, ed., *The New American Right* (New York, 1955 [republished as *The Radical Right:*

"The New American Right" Expanded and Updated (New York, 1964)]).

For earlier studies of the bases of McCarthy's support offering results generally similar to Rogin's and criticizing Bell *et. al.*, see Martin Trow, "Small Businessmen, Political Tolerance, and Support for McCarthy," *American Journal of Sociology,* LXIV (November 1958), 270-281; Nelson W. Polsby, "Towards an Explanation of McCarthyism," *Political Studies*, VIII (October 1960), 250-271.

85. Rogin, *McCarthy*, 221, 222, 225, 103, 248.

86. *Ibid.*, 253, 254. Rogin suggests a liberal role but does not put it so strongly as I have here, 256.

87. *Ibid.*, 278, 279, 282.

88. Michael Rogin, "Wallace and the Middle Class: The White Backlash in Wisconsin," *Public Opinion Quarterly*, XXX (Spring 1966), 98-108 (quotation at 100).

89. J. David Valaik, "Catholics, Neutrality, and the Spanish Embargo, 1937-1939," *Journal of American History*, LIV (June 1967), 73-85.

90. See Sidney Verba, *et. al.*, "Public Opinion and the War in Vietnam," *American Political Science Review*, LXI (June 1967), 318.

91. *Ibid.*, 320. For a bizarre misreading by a pluralist journal which concludes from the same data that pressure from below for escalation was increasing, see "Current Reading" (apparently written by Irving Kristol or Daniel Bell), *The Public Interest*, number 11 (Spring 1968), 89.

92. *New York Times*, March 17, 1966; quoted in Verba *et. al.*, "Public Opinion and Vietnam," 322.

93. Many other instances which do not fit the pluralists' portrayal of popular conservatism could be cited, for example: the Dearborn, Michigan anti-war referendum of 1966; the California right-to-work referendum of 1958; the responsible conduct of the Chicago electorate on referenda (Theodore J. Lowi, "Machine Politics—Old and New," *The Public Interest*, number 9 [Fall 1967], 91-92); the 1962 "anti-subversive" Francis Amendment in California (see Rogin, "Wallace," 106n.)

94. Martin Trow, "Small Businessmen," 270, describes the essays in *The New American Right* as "based on almost no empirical evidence at all, at least so far as their efforts to explain the popular support of these [conservative] movements are concerned." Polsby, "Towards an Explanation of McCarthyism," 254-256, offers similar criticisms.

95. Irving Kristol, "Historians and the Idea of Democracy," paper delivered at 1969 meeting of Organization of American Historians.

96. Rogin concludes that pluralism "may best be judged" as a venture into conservative theory rather than "as the product of science" (*McCarthy*, 282).

97. Bell, "Passion and Politics," 61.

98. Kristol, "Historians and the Idea of Democracy," 26.

99. Reprinted in Schlesinger, *Politics of Hope*, 5, 9, 18, 19.

100. Niebuhr, *Irony*, 163, 166, 164.

101. *Ibid.*, 112, 113, 115. LaFeber, *America, Russia, and the Cold War*, 133.

102. C. Wright Mills, "On the New Left," *Studies on the Left*, II (1961), number 1, 64-65.

IV

103. United States, House of Representatives, Committee on Un-American Activities, 83rd Cong., 1st Sess., *Communist Methods of Infiltration (Education)*, Part I, 47, 53, 56. Boorstin had previously testified in executive session, apparently during the summer of 1951 (see *ibid.*, s1), and I have been unable to locate any record of that testimony.

104. *Ibid.*, 59, 60, 49. Boorstin has acknowledged membership in the Party "for a period of something less than a year. . . That is about 14 years ago that my association ceased" (48). "It was not an important episode in my life. . . ." (49).

105. *Ibid.*, 51.

106. Through the Hillel Foundation at the University of Chicago (*ibid.*, 51).

107. *Ibid.*, 52.

108. *Ibid.*, 60.

109. *The Saturday Review*, February 6, 1954, 7.

110. *Ibid.*, 48. Nevins said more or less the same thing in talks to a gathering of American History teachers at Stanford in August of 1951 and to the Society of American Archivists at Dearborn, Michigan, September 14, 1953 (see *ibid.*, 7; Edward N. Saveth, "What Historians Teach about Business," *Fortune*, April 1952, 118; Allan Nevins, "New Lamps for Old in History," *American Archivist*, XVII [January 1954], 3-12 [from which Nevins adapted his *Saturday Review* article]). For a warning against "overcorrection," see *Fortune*, September 1951, 83.

111. Nevins, "Should American History be Rewritten?" 47-49.

112. Debating with Nevins, Matthew Josephson saw a touch of 1984 in Nevins' arguments and asked, "Will the New History of this country [like that of Germany and the Soviet Union], too, be rewritten as crude propaganda for the party in power?" He saw in Nevins' history a "big-business version of the American Century," and he thought Nevins' call to rewrite history "ill timed" when anti-communism was making it all the more difficult to talk about possible flaws in the American past. (*Ibid.*, 10, 46).

113. *American Historical Review*, LVI (January 1951), 261-275; reprinted with a few changes in Samuel Eliot Morison, *By Land and By Sea* (New York, 1953), 346-359. (Citations below are to version in *American Historical Review*.)

114. *Ibid.*, 265-270. For a claim that Morison misrepresented Beard, see Howard K. Beale, "The Professional Historian: His Theory and His Practice," *Pacific Historical Review*, XXII (August 1953), 251.

115. Morison, "Faith," 266-273. By December of 1968, Morison had apparently forgotten his earlier admonition when he complained that "most history textbooks are smooth as grease. They avoid the conflicts and disorders that have taken place in our past." In the same interview, Morison told the *New York Times* (December 16, 1968), "We should regard the black people as potential good citizens and make a place for them in the power structure." (The racism of earlier editions of the Morison and Commager textbook, *The Growth of the American Republic*, is notorious. For examples, see a pamphlet published by black students at New York's City College in 1950 and reprinted by Queens College Committee on Democracy in Education; Leo Field, "Morison and Commager vs. Negro History," *New Foundations*, IV (November 1950), 10-12.

116. But for some sensible criticisms, see Beale, "Professional Historian," 251-252. Another call for what might be called an "applied history" echoed Morison's. Aiming not so much at the red menace as at Harry Truman, Saveth, "What Historians Teach about Business," urged a "conservative synthesis" in order "to challenge the Fair Deal influence in historical writing, and at the polls as well" (174).

117. Oscar Handlin, Arthur Meier Schlesinger, Samuel Eliot Morison, Frederick Merk, Arthur Meier Schlesinger, Jr., Paul Herman Buck, *Harvard Guide to American History* (Cambridge, 1955), 12. (For the authorship of individual sections, see ix).

118. Not considered here, although of great importance, are innumerable ways in which the *Harvard Guide* is a political document. Consider, for example, the blatant political bias in the selection of 1) magazines

and newspapers as "historical sources" for the recent period (172-173, 177 and 2) "opportunities for research"; consider especially exclusions from the list (37).

119. *Ibid.*, 12.
120. *ibid.*, 49. Morison's remarks here are derived from his "History as a Literary Art: An Appeal to Young Historians," Old South Association, Leaflet, Series II, no. 1 (Boston, [1946?]).
121. Harvey Breit, "Talk with Mr. Schlesinger," *New York Times Book Review*, September 18, 1949, 19.
122. Arthur Mann, "The Progressive Tradition" in John Higham, ed., *The Reconstruction of American History* (New York, 1962), 174. To the writer these remarks convey a special irony, since Mann was on the committee which reached the decision to dismiss me from the University of Chicago because my "convictions" allegedly interfered with my scholarship.
123. Conyers, Read, "The Social Responsibilities of the Historian," *American Historical Review*, LV (January 1950), 275, 281-284.
124. See Beale, "Professional Historian," 254. For an acknowledgment that historians had "relaxed their skepticism," together with a denial, in apparent response to Read, that historians "have been enlisted, like physicists, in the cold war," see Arthur M. Schlesinger, Jr., *Politics of Hope*, 52. Schlesinger continues, "there has been neither the effort to do this on the part of government nor the desire on the part of the profession" (*ibid.*).
125. Higham, "Beyond Consensus," 609,616,619-625. It goes without saying that Higham was not responsible for the renovation; for an instance of hostility toward him on the part of a leading consensus historian, see Oscar Handlin, "Communication," *Mississippi Valley Historical Review*, XLIX (September 1962), 408.

V

126. The following glimpse into the writing of history is only that; it is far from a complete survey of all the history written since World War II. But I believe that it is more than merely impressionistic. It covers a wide range chronologically and topically, and it deals with authors who will generally be conceded to be among what one of them once called the "pacesetters" of the profession. This does not mean that it was the only kind of history being written at the time. But unless — in the style of the 'fifties — we refuse to acknowledge the possibility of generalizing, I believe that it will be conceded that what follows

represents the dominant trend in the writing of American history in the period.

127. Daniel J. Boorstin, *The Americans: The Colonial Experience* (New York, 1968), 1. My reading of Boorstin has been influenced by remarks on Boorstin and other consensus historians in John Higham's two landmark articles, "The Cult of the 'American Consensus,'" and "Beyond Consensus."

In this and the subsequent volume of *The Americans (The National Experience* [New York, 1965]) Boorstin acknowledges the support given him by the Relm Foundation. This organization has also supported the Hoover Institution on War, Revolution, and Peace, the Georgetown Centre for Strategic Studies, Gerhard Niemeyer and Robert Strausz-Hupé. For more on the Foundation and the anti- communist crusades of its director, see Judith Coburn, "I Wonder Who's Kissinger Now?" *Mayday*, December 20-27, 1968, 4.

128. Boorstin, *Americans: Colonial Experience*, 29. Boorstin felt that Perry Miller often took the Puritan distinctions "more seriously and more precisely" than did the Puritans themselves (380). Although Miller may be vulnerable to the claim that he allowed the theology of an elite to stand for the thought of the many, this is not what Boorstin meant. Puritan orthodoxy, Boorstin said, had a "peculiar character"; the Puritans were "less interested in theology itself, than in the application of theology to everyday life"(5). Boorstin's evidence was often unpersuasive: he might describe Puritan sermons as a form of entertainment (14), a way of "passing the time" (3) in an era before television and movies (14), but we have no more evidence of this than we have evidence that the Pope reads his beads for kicks. That the Puritans saw biblical parallels for even the most trivial of everyday events (19) seems more nearly evidence that they were deeply theological than that, as Boorstin seems to contend, the end of ideology was Puritan dogma.

129. *Ibid.*, 9.

130. *Ibid.*, 35-37.

131. *ibid.*, 68, 67, 34, 63, 47; for an alternative view, see several essays in Frederick B. Tolles, *Quakers and the Atlantic Culture* (New York, 1960), especially "The Culture of Early Pennsylvania," 114-131.

132. Boorstin, *Americans: Colonial Experience*, 58, 54, 55.

133. *Ibid.*, 96, 80, 88, 71. Cf. Daniel J. Boorstin, *The Image of What Happened to the American Dream* (Harmondsworth, England, 1963), where the term "extravagant expectations" is used to express essentially Burkean ideals.

134. Related themes to be found in *Americans: Colonial Experience* are American exceptionalism and superiority and the implacable hostility of the enemy—in this instance, the Indian. Also, the evils of cosmopolitanism: Boorstin quotes Jefferson likening the Quakers to the Jews or the Jesuits, while himself calling these utopian ideologues "a kind of international conspiracy." (64).

135. *Idem, The Americans: National Experience*, 399.

136. *American Political Science Review*, XLV (December 1951), 1086-1099.

137. *Ibid.*, 1096,1086, 1098, 1095, 1099, 1089.

138. *Ibid.*, 1086, 1097.

139. More recently, writing of the making of the Pennsylvania Constitution of 1776, David Hawke has paid his respects directly to Hoffer. That constitution, reflecting the thought which John Adams found "too democratical" in Paine's *Common Sense*, was put over by "a small band of men," says Hawke in *In the Midst of a Revolution* (Philadelphia, 1961), 13. These men refused to face the fact that humans are not very "malleable" (197) and tried "to translate theory into fact" (190). Hawke describes the six key men in this operation—Paine is one of them—variously as failures, bankrupts, men with marital and other family troubles (103-104); one, about whom Hawke admits little is known, is thus described as "quietly teaching school, not once creating a public stir" and therefore "slowly accumulating a bitter feeling toward the world around him"! (105). All six "had reason to be discontent with themselves and with the way the world had treated them" (103):

> Each believed his talents were going to waste, unrecognized by society. Each detested the present and found happiness only in the future. . . . Out of the depths of their frustration and faith in the future emerged their passionate attachment to independence. And out of their innocence developed their common belief that this perfect world would come quickly, instantly once evil had been crushed. (106)

Hoffer, whose work Hawke tells us is indispensable to an understanding of the American Revolution, is called in to explain this bizarre conduct:

> The craving to change the world [Hawke quotes Hoffer] is perhaps a reflection of the craving to change ourselves. The sick in soul insist that it is humanity that is sick, and they are the surgeons to operate on it (103).

140. Neibuhr, *Irony*, 30.

141. Forrest McDonald, *The Formation of the American Republic, 1776-1790* (Baltimore, 1965), 235-236. This passage was brought to my attention by Staughton Lynd, *Class Conflict, Slavery, and the United States Constitution: Ten Essays* (Indianapolis, 1967), 7.

132

142. Kenyon, "Where Paine Went Wrong," 1095-1096.
   The preceding account of course only scratches the surface of the
   present- mindedness of recent historiography of early America. It
   should also be noted that the interpretation of mass conduct in the
   American Revolution which focuses on manipulation and skilful
   propaganda is essentially a conspiracy theory. See the discussion of
   Hawke, immediately above, for one such instance; more generally,
   see Jesse Lemisch, "The American Revolution Seen From the
   Bottom Up" in Bernstein, *Towards a New Past*, 3-45.
143. Stanley M. Elkins, *Slavery: A Problem in American Institutional
   and Intellectual Life* (New York, 1963 [1st ed., Chicago, 1959]). My
   perception of the abolitionists in the following discussions of Elkins
   and Schlesinger has been influenced by Martin B. Duberman, "The
   Abolitionists and Psychology," *Journal of Negro History*, XLVII
   (July 1962), 183-191.
144. Elkins, *Salvery*, 158, 157, 141, 146-147.
145. *Ibid.*, 141, 147.
146. *Ibid.*, 147-148.
147. *Ibid.*, 161, 150-151, 176.
148. *Ibid.*, 156.
149. *Ibid.*, 151-152.
150. *Ibid.*, 158, 164, 161. For an illuminating discussion of the meaning of
   "guilt" as an abolitionist motive, see Duberman, "Abolitionists and
   Psychology." Duberman notes that "Under the Freudian micros-
   cope, it would be a rare man indeed whose life showed no evidence of
   pathological behaviour" (186). "But an individual's public involvement is never completely explained by discussing his private
   pathology" (188).
151. Elkins, *Slavery*, 36.
152. *Ibid.*, 185, 188, 188n., 189n. Underlying these anti-radical attitudes is
   the complex of conservative values associated with end of ideology:
   a Neibuhrian pessimism about man and his nature, and about social
   change, doubts about human perfectibility and equality (see, for
   example, 85, 153, 160, 169-170). At bottom, Elkins subscribes to
   'fifties notions of the intractability of human nature, and it is this
   theme which links his consideration of the abolitionists to his
   examination of the social psychology of the salve. The abolitionists,
   says Elkins, erroneously "thought that nothing could actually be
   said about the Negro's 'true' nature because that nature was veiled
   by the institution of slavery. It could only be revealed by tearing
   away the veil" (83). Cf. Weisstein, "Woman as Nigger":
   It is obvious that a study of human behaviour requires a study of the social

contexts in which people move, the expectations as to how they will
behave, and the authority that tells them who they are and what they are
supposed to do. . .
  Except for their genitals, I don't know what immutable differences
exist between men and women. Perhaps there are some other unchange-
able differences; probably there are a number of irrelevant differences.
But it is clear that until social expectations for men and women are equal,
until we provide equal respect for both sexes, answers to this question
will simply reflect our prejudices. [58]

153. *Partisan Review*, XVI (October 1949), 969-981. Citations below are
   to the essay as it appeared in *Politics of Hope*, 35-47.
154. *Ibid.*, 37-38.
155. *Ibid.*, 38.
156. See Jesse Lemisch, "Who Won the Civil War, Anyway?" *The
   Nation*, April 8, 1961, 300-302; this article is, in part, derivative from
   Schlesinger.
157. Schlesinger, *Politics of Hope*, 45, 39.
158. *Ibid.*, 41-42. 46-47; *idem, Vital Centre*, 254.
159. *Idem, Politics of Hope*, 105; *Vital Centre*, 159, 38, 37.
160. *Ibid.*, 77; *Politics of Hope*, 39, 43,
161. *Ibld.*, 39; *Vital Centre*, xxii, 65, 98.
162. *Politics of Hope*, 43; *Vital Centre*, 10.
163. Pollack, "Fear of Man," 2. (Bobbs-Merrill Reprint)
164. *Ibid.*, 3, 4, 7, 8.
165. Oscar Handlin, "Reconsidering the Populists," *Agricultural
   History*, XXXIX (April 1965), 10, 11, 12.
166. Irwin Unger, "Critique of Norman Pollack's 'Fear of Man'," *ibid.*,
   17.
167. While not finding the Populists revolutionary (*McCarthy*, 186),
   Rogin offers much evidence in support of Pollack on the nature of
   Populism. Considering the Populist tendency to explain certain
   events as conspiracies, Rogin notes that conspiracies *did* occur and
   that the Populists' "perception of courthouse 'rings' making political
   decisions was close to the truth" (172). Rogin notes that Hofstadter
   supports the contention that the Populists were jingoists by finding
   evidence of jingoism in Populist areas—without noting that his
   evidence may be coming from the Populists' opponents (177, 318).
   Rogin often finds among the Populists' opponents "apocalyptic,
   conspiratorial, and utopian preoccupations" (56; see also 170, 171n.,
   177, 315).
168. Schlesinger, *Vital Centre*, 44.
169. Allan Nevins, *Study in Power: John D. Rockefeller, Industrialist and
   Philanthropist* (2 vols.; New York, 1953).
170. *Ibid.*, I, viii-ix. Cf. Schlesinger, *Vital Centre*, 44:

> . . . to save the nation from the "robber barons," would the Doughface reduce our industrial capacity to the point where it was when the "robber barons" came on the scene? . . . the price we paid [for industrialization], though perhaps exorbitant, was infintely less in human terms than the price paid by the people of Russia. . . .

171. Allan Nevins, *John D. Rockefeller, The Heroic Age of American Enterprise* (2 vols.; New York, 1940), II, 721.

172. Nevins, *Study in Power*, II, 480. Emphasis added.

173. Aptheker, *Laureates*, 37.

174. Rogin, *McCarthy*, 292.

175. Allan Nevins, "What Leadership Means in a Democracy," *New York Times Magazine*, November 17, 1957, 11. For more cold-war journalism by Nevins, see his "Tyrannies Must Fall," *Collier's*, October 20, 1951, 16 ff.

176. Schlesinger, *Politics of Hope*, 18.

177. Thomas A. Bailey, *The Man in the Street: The Impact of American Public Opinion on Foreign Policy* (New York, 1948), 13.

178. Henry Steele Commager, "Presidential Power: The Issue Analyzed," *New York Times Magazine*, January 14, 1951, 11.

179. *Ibid.*, and "Does the President Have Too Much Power?", *ibid.*, April 1, 1951, 15 ff.

180. Commager, "Presidential Power," 11.

181. *Ibid.*

182. *Idem*, "Does the President Have Too Much Power?" 15.

183. *Ibid.*, 35, 33.

184. In connection with cold war revisionism of another sort, the *New York Times*, December 14, 1951, describes Frances Friedman's *An Outline of American History* as "the outstanding best-seller of the State Department, with 2,400,000 copies distributed thus far . . . [all apparently outside of the U.S.]. It was reviewed by Dr. Wood Gray of George Washington University and the final chapter was rewritten by Dr. Richard Hofstadter of Columbia University to adapt it more closely to the more recent United States aims in Germany." I have been unable to obtain a copy of this publication.

185. Henry Steele Commager, "Analysis of the American Character," *New York Times Magazine*, January 2, 1949, 5. For some more recent assertions reflecting the same assumptions, see *idem*, "The Ambiguous American," *ibid.*, May 3, 1964, 16 ff ("Notwithstanding the massive denial of equality to the Negro, and to other colored peoples as well, equality is still the greatest common denominator of the American character" [*ibid.*, 144]; this is true only because Commager has chosen a perspective which *defines* it as true).

186. As an undergraduate in the field at Yale (B.A., 1957), I recall much

class time and reading devoted to definition and justification of "American Studies." My strongest recollection of the content which I was taught in undergraduate seminars relate to American abundance, homogeneity, social mobility, the "culture concept," and——especially in discussion of Ortega y Gasset, the mass media, and foreign policy—a tremendous condescension in attitudes toward popular judgment and democracy. In the summer of 1957, just after graduation, I recall the astonishment with which I discovered, as a hitch-hiker, that people in one-newspaper towns in the Pacific Northwest had sufficient intellectual resources to laugh at those newspapers when they ridiculed public power as "socialistic"; and my undergraduate education had ill prepared me for both the title and the substance of an article which I saw in a magazine for sale in a Cleveland bus station: Harvey Swados, "The Myth of the Happy Worker," *The Nation*, August 17, 1957, 65-68.

For some of American Studies' literature of definition, see Tremaine McDowell, *American Studies* (Minneapolis, 1948); Robert H. Walker, *American Studies in the United States: A Survey of College Programs* (Baton Rouge, 1958); Edward F. Grier, "Programs in American Civilization," *Journal of Higher Education*, XXV (April 1954), 179-190; *American Quarterly* (21 vols. to date; Spring 1949-   ). Studies need to be done on the financing of American Studies and, in general on the increased availability of funds for various projects which, while doubtless valuable, clearly have political meaning (for instance, the publication of the papers of various past American political leaders). See also the increased interest in the place of U.S. history in the college curriculum: "Study of U.S. History Gains as More Colleges Require It," *New York Times*, April 17, 1950, 1 ff.

187. David M. Potter, *People of Plenty: Economic Abundance and the American Character* (Chicago, 1954), 117-118, 84. For end of ideology, see 121-122; for a benevolent view of American relations with Latin America, see 130-131.
188. Henry Steele Commager, "Analysis of the American Character," 5.
189. *Idem*, "The U.S. in 1970—Three Forecasts," *New York Times Magazine*, May 17, 1959, 76.
190. *Idem*, "Brave World of the Year 2000," *ibid*., November 1, 1959, 26.
191. Schlesinger, *Vital Centre*, 33n. See also above for Schlesinger's prediction of increasing rigidity in the U.S.S.R.
192. *Ibid*., 24.
193. *Ibid*., 190.
194. Commager, "U.S. in 1970," 76; "Brave World," 26, 28, 30, 32.
195. Allan Nevins, "U.S. in 1970," 25.

196. Staughton Lynd, "Beyond Beard," in Bernstein, *Towards a New Past*, 49.
197. Bell, "Passion and Politics," 59.
198. Kenyon, "Where Paine Went Wrong," 1098.
199. Lemisch, "American Revolution from the Bottom Up," 10-15.
200. See, for instance, Leonard D. White, *The Federalists: A Study in Administrative History* (New York, 1959); *idem, The Jeffersonians: A Study in Administrative History, 1801-1829* (New York, 1951). The latter concludes:

> . . . .the republicans brought no revolution in administration. They found a system in full order . . . and it was taken over with hardly a ripple and maintained substantially intact for over a quarter century [546] . . .
> . . . One circumstance of special importance was the uninterrupted control of government and the administrative system after 1801 by gentlemen. The same social class that had set up the new system in 1789 carried it forward. . . . The basic outlook, predispositions, habits, and ways of life of men in the public service were unchanged; and the ethical standards of the civil servants of 1820 were identical with those of 1800. [548] . . .

201. For one amusing item of documentation from a nonpluralist, see Gabriel Kolko's quotation of an exchange between Henry Clay Frick and Andrew Carnegie on the election of 1892: "I am very sorry for President Harrison," wrote Frick, "but I cannot see that our interests are going to be affected one way or the other by the change in administration." Carnegie replied: "Cleveland! Landslide! Well we have nothing to fear and perhaps it is best. People will now think the Protected Manfrs. will be attended to and quit agitating. Cleveland is pretty good fellow. Off for Venice tomorrow" (*The Triumph of Conservatism: A Reinterpretation of American History, 1900-1916* [Chicago, 1967], 62-63).

VI

202. Andrew Kopkind, "The Future-Planners," *New Republic*, February 25, 1967; here cited from reprint in *American Psychologist*, XXII (November 1967), 1036-1041. Bell subsequently headed a task force for presidential candidate Hubert Humphrey on "The Future": *Village Voice*, August 1, 1968, 3.
203. Quoted in Kopkind, "Future-Planners," 1036.
204. "Liberal Anti-Communism Revisited," 42.
205. *New York Times*, October 28, 1968, 2; *ibid.*, December 4, 1968, 62.
    At the same time, Irving Kristol's publishing firm brought out Talcott Parsons' collection of essays by Lipset, Bendix, and others,

originating in a Voice of America series. A reviewer in *Science* called it a "self-congratulatory celebration," "a hymn of thanksgiving for America the affluent, and a benediction for a modern society in which the traditional distinctions between ruler and ruled are allegedly no more": Talcott Parsons, ed., *American Sociology: Perspectives, Problems, Methods* (New York, 1968); reviewed by Alvin W. Gouldner in *Science*, 162 (October 11, 1968), 247-249.

206. *New York Times*, October 26, 1968, 65.

207. *Ibid.*, May 10, 1969.

208. Frank Donner, "The Colleges Play Ball," *The Nation*, August 11, 1969, 112.

209. For some interesting comments on coercive aspects of end of ideology, see Conor Cruise O'Brien, review of Chaim I. Waxman, ed., *The End of Ideology Debate* in *New York Times Book Review*, February 16, 1969, 12.

210. *Chicago Tribune*, January 31, 1969, 1; February 1, 1969, 2; *New York Times*, February 1, 1969; *Chicago Sun-Times*, February 16, 1969, section 2, 2; *Time*, September 5, 1969, 58.

211. *Chicago Today*, August 27, 1969.

212. James Petras, "Berkeley and the New Conservative Backlash," *New Left Review*, number 31 (May-June, 1965), 62. For a description of sit-inners at the University of Chicago as "coprophilac," see statement by Physiology Professor Elwood U. Jensen, February 10, 1969 (mimeographed; distributed by University of Chicago).

213. Lewis S. Feuer, *The Conflict of Generations: The Character and Significance of Student Movements* (New York, 1969). See also Joseph Schwab, *College Curriculum and Student Protest* (Chicago, 1969).

214. *Ibid.*, 16; Franklin L. Ford of Harvard, *New York Times*, April 12, 1968, 18; editorial, *ibid.*, December 27, 1968; Anthropology Professor Milton Singer in speech to sit-in, University of Chicago Administration Building, May 1966; *Chicago Sun-Times*, February 16, 1969, section 2, 1-2; *Chicago Maroon*, May 9, 1969, 7.

215. Petras, "Berkeley," 62-63.

216. Professor Charles Huggins: see *Chicago Maroon*, May 9, 1969, 7. A recording of his press conference of February 6, 1969, was broadcast by a Chicago radio station. Adolph A. Berle has had the same insight: *New York Times*, July 17, 1969.

217. *New York Times*, April 12, 1969, 18. Cf. Lemisch, "American Revolution from the Bottom Up," 25.

218. Petras, "Berkeley," 60.

219. *Commentary*, XLVI (July 1968), 38.

138

220. *New York Times*, May 10, 1969.
221. *New York Times*, April 4, 1969, 1, 18; *Civil Liberties*, June, 1969, 4. Four lawyers in the New York Civil Liberties Union dissented, saying that the statement would "add the voice of the A.C.L.U. to the repressive forces already at work against social change in our society . . . (*New York Times*, April 6, 1969, 51).
222. Personal experience, April 1969.
223. See *New York Times*, April 1, 1967.
224. Louis Joughin, ed., *Academic Freedom and Tenure: A Handbook of the American Association of University Professors* (Madison, 1967), 132, 134, 133.
225. President R. A. Weil of Roosevelt University, mentioned in statement by J.J. Roth *et. al.*, on Lynd case, April 22, 1968 (mimeographed).
226. Joughin, *Academic Freedom*, 7, 136-137.
227. Conversation with Louis Joughin at American Historical Association Annual Meeting, New York, 1966.
228. Bertram H. Davis to Alfred Young, October 31, 1968, quoted in Alfred Young, Christopher Lasch, *et. al.* to Bertram H. Davis, March 17, 1969, 3 (mimeographed). As of October 1969, the AAUP has taken no further action on the case.
229. Experience of Marvin L. Michael Kay, who was an associate professor at Alfred University when these events took place (May 1968). In February of 1969 the AAUP's observer recognized a *prima facie* breach of academic freedom, but Professor Kay has since heard nothing further from the national organization.
230. See below. More recently, the same man has equated the conduct of students sitting in with that of Minute Men who invaded the sit-in and assaulted students: statement by Professor James E. Miller, Jr., February 9, 1969 (mimeographed and distributed by University of Chicago).
231. *New York Times*, editorial, June 16, 1969; see also editorial, *ibid.*, September 23, 1969: "A strengthening of the vital centre is imperative to the pacification as well as the reform of the campuses."
232. *Ibid.*, August 6, 1969, 16.
233. Donner, "Colleges Play Ball," 114 also describes cooperation by CCNY, Brooklyn College, Cornell, Harvard, University of California, Stanford.
234. *New York Times*, August 21, 1969.
235. *Ibid.*, editorial, November 1, 1967.
236. Edith Green, for instance; see Andrew Kopkind, "Green Stuff," *Hard Times*, May 19-26, 1969.

237. Hans J. Morgenthau, "What Ails America," *New Republic*, October 28, 1967, 21; Morgenthau *et. al.*, "Academic Freedom, Autonomy and Protest," November 2, 1967 (mimeographed; circulated to University of Chicago faculty by Secretary of the Faculties).

238. Abe Fortas, *Concerning Dissent and Civil Disobedience* (New York, 1968), vi.

239. *Daily Northwestern*, October 3, 1969, 1; *Roosevelt Torch*, September 29, 1969, 4; *Chicago Maroon*, August 21, 1969, 1, 5; *New York Times*, August 17, 1969, 52; *Hard Times*, September 29-October 6, 1969, 1-4; *Chicago Journalism Review*, II (February 1969), 8; *Chicago Sun-Times*, August 8, 1969.

240. For instance, University of Chicago, May 1966; Northwestern University, May 1969.

241. See, for instance, Hanry W. DeZutter, "I Was a Campus Spy for the FBI," *Chicago Daily News*, May 12, 1969.

242. Personal experience, Northwestern University, November 1968.

243. For instance, at the University of Chicago 1969 sit-in.

244. Technically, off-campus; shot Thursday May 15, 1969, died Monday, May 19, 1969: *Ramparts*, August 1969, 58-59.

    Hoffer cannot be held directly responsible for this event. But, so long as we believe that ideas have consequences, we must assume that there is some sort of connection between murder by university and municipal officials and the incitement of university and municipal officials to murder. Recommendations by a nationally known member of a presidential commission, who is a research professor at the University of California, legitimize the conduct which he recommends, no matter how barbaric that conduct may be.

245. *Chicago Maroon*, May 6, 1969, 1, 3.

246. The Chicago police conducted the investigation in accord with *their* ideology; they announced that they had a list of forty-three suspects —the students who had been expelled for sitting in over the firing of sociology professor Marlene Dixon. Six months later, no one has been brought to trial. (For an attempt to murder historian Herbert Aptheker, see "Anti-Red Bomb Plotter in Bronx Gets 2 Years," *New York Times*, February 6, 1968, 20: "Police experts said that the blast had actually been timed for his [Aptheker's] appearance, but had occurred late because of faulty construction."

247. University of Chicago, "Report on Disciplinary and Appeals Decisions," April 8, 1969 (mimeographed). The University of Chicago had suspended fifty-eight students in 1967.

248. As Left political activities are more and more openly defined as "unprofessional conduct," there are fewer and fewer arguments

about whether a particular dismissal was "political." The files of the New University Conference contain extensive records of political firings and suspensions. For a few cases in addition to those mentioned elsewhere in this paper, see *Guardian*, September 13, 1969 (Dartmouth and Tulane); *ibid.*, October 4, 1969 and *New York Times*, September 21, 1969, 48 (U.C.L.A.); *Newsweek*, September 22, 1969, 60 (Harvard).

249. Report in *The Chronicle of Higher Education*, summarized in *Guardian*, September 13, 1969, 5.

VII

250. Statement, February 7, 1969 (mimeographed and distributed by University of Chicago); see also statements by S. William Halperin (February 6), John Hope Franklin (February 7), and Richard C. Wade (February 12).

251. The Committee asked such questions as "Do you believe in the demands of the sit-in" "Do you believe in the tactics of the sit-in?" "How did you vote at political meetings outside the building?" "What is your conception of the University?" "Do you still feel the same way about the sit-in as you did then?" For the Committee's statement of its criteria, see University of Chicago, "Report of Disciplinary Actions," March 17, 1969 (mimeographed). Careful studies by a group of graduate students in the social sciences led to the conclusion that "for any given level of participation in the sit-in, those students with radical political views received much more punitive treatment than moderate students": *Spartacus*, March 12, May 1, 1969. According to notes of an official student observer of the disciplinary committee, Mann, who viewed the sit-in as "part of a power struggle," was "the most instrumental in preventing those who disagreed with the aims of the sit-in but who frequented the building in hopes of persuading people to leave from being very severely disciplined, whatever the duration of their stay had been." One student connected the Committee's conduct with the subsequent assault on Flacks: "If the respectable and powerful people in a society can punish people for their political atitudes, then why can't an ordinary citizen take upon himself the same prerogative?" David C. Brown, letter to the editor, *Chicago Maroon*, May 9, 1969, 7.

252. See David Applebaum *et. al., The Case For Abolishing ROTC* (Boston, 1969), 19-20. For Seymour Martin Lipset's proposal, see *ibid.*, 19.

253. Arthur Schlesinger, Jr., "When, If Ever, Do You Call In the Cops?" *New York Times Magazine*, May 4, 1969, 35.

254. *New York Times*, January 26, 1969, and various items in mailings from the Coordinating Centre for Democratic Opinion, dated February 10, 1969 and from UCRA, dated May 5, 1969.

255. Jerry L. Avorn, *et. al., Up Against the Ivy Wall: A History of The Columbia Crisis* (New York, 1968), 149, 212, 214, 215, 279-280. *New York Times*, June 5, 1968, 34. For the pro-administration roles of Fritz Stern and William Leuchtenburg, see Avorn, *Up Against The Ivy Wall*, 155, 210, 213, 218.

256. *New York Times*, May 29, 1969, 18; *Columbia Chronicle*, April-May, 1969; mailing from Columbia to alumni, June 20, 1969. Cordier offered praise of the faculty advertisement in his testimony before the Senate Permanent Subcommittee on Investigations, August 5, 1969, and asked that the ad be read into the record (*Columbia Chronicle*, September 1969, 2). In his testimony Cordier made it clear that separating SDS from the moderates was a central element of his strategy for "containing" and "defusing." The handing over of SDS names is clearly a part of that strategy.

257. Statement by President Beadle, April 11, 1967 (mimeographed); *Chicago Maroon*, April 14, 1967, 1, 5, April 18, 1967, 1, May 2, 1967, 4. The faculty member in question rapidly clammed up publicly while privately humbling himself before the right people, delivered a sort of a "Checkers Speech," suggested others were to blame, and emerged from the affair relatively unscathed.

258. "If we may indulge in exaggeration to emphasize the distinction we are struggle for, the first category of offenses might be assimilated to 'treason', the second to nuisance" (University of Chicago, Kalven Committee to Review Disciplinary Procedures," February 24, 1969 [mimeographed]). As has been indicated above, the quotation marks around "treason" were in effect removed by a disciplinary committee which inquired into students' conceptions of the university. It is one of the central points of this paper that when liberals choose to define certain crimes as treason, no matter how they qualify it, repeated past experience indicates that their label gives licence to others to use the term without qualification.

259. I have used the version published in *Chicago Sun-Times*, section two, November 6, 1966, 6.

260. Daniel J. Boorstin, Commencement Address at University of Tulsa, June 1, 1969 (mimeographed).

261. *Idem*, "Dissent: A Destructive Spirit Stalking the Nation," a nationally-syndicated article which appeared in *Chicago Sun-Times*,

November 12, 1967, section 2, 3.

262. *Life* quoted this passage in its editorial, "Honest Dissent vs. Ugly Disorder," November 10, 1967, 4.

263. See *idem*, "Dissent, Dissension and the News," a fuller version of the speech described above, published in *The University of Chicago Magazine*, March 1968, 16-19. It says something, too, of the "political neutrality" of one of our major universities that the University of Chicago chose to reprint this speech in its alumni magazine. A few months before, SDS members had left in seats before Boorstin's class leaflets which excerpted his HUAC testimony (described above) and which, while noting that he had a right to his political opinions, questioned the appropriateness of firing me for allegedly allowing my convictions to interfere with my scholarship in the light of Boorstin's boast of the inter-relations between *his* convictions and his scholarship. (For the leaflet, see *Radical America*, I [November-December 1967], 59-61). The university responded by labeling the leaflet "scurrilous" and condemning "invasion or disruption" of the classroom "by outsiders." (Statement of Social Science Divisional Executive Committee, University of Chicago, October 21, 1967 [mimeograph]). Boorstin was promoted to Preston and Sterling Morton Distinguished Service Professor, but he subsequently chose to move to the Smithsonian Institution, where he now sees making "history seem contemporary" as "the challenge for all historians . . .": *Chicago Sun-Times*, October 19, 1969, 24.

264. AHA Annual Meeting, New York City, 1968, "Professional Organizations and Political Issues."

265. Mayoralty campaign, 1967. Other signers included Hans J. Morgenthau, Louis Gottschalk, Arthur Mann, William McNeill, John B. Wolf. I doubt that the AAUP would expend much energy in my defense if I allowed a photograph of myself teaching class at Roosevelt to circulate under the title, "Faculty for Fidel."

266. In the present, an interview with Wade was used to help make Daley's case in Chicago's official television version of the Democratic Convention Riots of 1968. (I am told that Wade was furious over the use of the interview, but he did not succeed in making his fury public. See Robert A. LeVine, letter to the editor, *Chicago Maroon*, November 28, 1968, 6. Wade's subsequent acceptance of a Daley appointment indicates that he must not have been too furious.)

267. Public Affairs Institute of Freedom House, *The United States and Eastern Asia* (pamphlet dated December 20, 1967), 3, 15, 16, 7, 5, 16, 8. Handlin was one of fourteen initiators.

268. *Ibid.*, 7, 15, 5, 17.
269. Gordon A. Craig, "Johannes von Müller: The Historian in Search of a Hero." *American Historical Review*, LXXIV (June 1969), 1498.
270. Irwin Ross, "Arthur Schlesinger Jr.," *New York Post*, April 3, 1961, 25. For a less gentle description, see Eugene McCarthy's comments on the occasion of the historian's defection to the Robert Kennedy campaign in 1968. McCarthy compared Schlesinger to a "mistletoe in a birch tree . . . You know mistletoe is the ultimate parasite;" *Chicago Sun Times*, March 17, 1968, 4.
271. Arthur M. Schlesinger, Jr., *A Thousand Days: John F. Kennedy in the White House* (Greenwich, Connecticut, 1967), 230-231.
272. *Ibid.*, 244.
273. *Ibid.*, 239.
274. Arthur M. Schlesinger, Jr., Letter to the editor, *New York Review of Books*, October 20, 1966, 37.
275. *Idem*, "The Origins of the Cold War," *Foreign Affairs*, XLVI (October 1967), 23n.
276. At the panel described above, note 264.
277. Arthur M. Schlesinger, Jr., "The Limits and Excesses of Presidential Power," *Saturday Review*, May 3, 1969, 17, 61, 62. Part way to his conversion, Schlesinger had written in 1966, ". . . the course of American history and the tempo of world change appear to have created an increasing demand for vigorous presidential leadership if the system is not to bog down in a morass of checks and balances." (Daniel J. Boorstin, ed., *An American Primer* [New York, 1968 (1st ed., Chicago, 1966)], 130.)
278. Robin Higham, review of Frederic J. Brown, *Chemical Warfare: A Study in Restraints, American Historical Review*, LXXIV (June 1969), 1583. (Cf. "U.S. Command in Saigon Rejects Pentagon View that Use of Tear Gas Reduces Civilian Casualties," *New York Times*, September 29, 1968, 11.)
279. Handlin's review is in *Mississippi Valley Historical Review*, XLVIII (March 1962), 743-744.
280. "Communication," *ibid.*, XLIX (September 1962), 407-408. For Handlin's *ad hominem* attack on Higham, see his "Communication," *ibid.*, 408.
281. *Journal of Southern History*, XXXV (February 1969), 77-80.
282. *New York Times Book Review*, May 12, 1968, 44.
283. *American Historical Review*, LXXIV (December 1968), 531-533.
284. *Journal of American History*, LV (September 1968), 369-371. This problem understandably interfered with Unger's perception: "Lemisch," he wrote, "is guilty of perpetrating another myth" in

depicting "proletarian heroes . . . engage[d] in 'guerilla warfare' against a conservative colonial elite who somehow resemble modern establishment liberals" (369-370). The closest I came to such remarks was in the suggestion that the struggle against the *British* used a "technique" that was "frequently that of guerilla warfare. . . . Although the analogy with guerilla warfare is only an analogy, it is suggestive. . . . Although an analogy with guerilla warfare can give us some suggestion as to the extent of patriotism during the Revolution, we need more specific information" (Lemisch, "American Revolution Seen From the Bottom Up," 26-27). The characterization of the Revolution as having a very qualified something in common with modern guerilla warfare is hardly either original or ludicrous. The contention that I saw colonials engaged in guerilla warfare against the colonial elite is an inexcuseable misreading, an instance of Unger's own failure "to play the scholarly game by the most elementary rules of fair play" (Unger, "New Left," 1262).

For another polemical review not mentioned above, see John L. Snell, "The Cold War: Four Contemporary Appraisals," *American Historical Review*, LXVIII (October, 1962), 69-75; cf. communications by D.F. Fleming and David Horowitz, *ibid.*, LXVIII (April 1963), 911-914. See also Daniel Boorstin's complaint that the American past "has come to be presented to more and more students as only so many centuries of Excedrin headaches" (Commencement Address, University of Tulsa, 1969).

285. John H. Mundy (one of the signers of "The University as a Sanctuary of Academic Freedom"), review of Robert E. Lerner, *The Age of Adversity: The Fourteenth Century, American Historical Review*, LXXIV (June 1969), 1606-1607. In fairness it should be noted that Mundy also suggested that the book in question might have gained something had it been more sensitive to some of the critical insights of "that otherwise damnable New Left . . .".

286. *AHA Newsletter*, VIII (October 1969), 1-14; see Ann Gordon's critique, to be published by the A.H.A.

287. *American Historical Review*, LXVII (January 1962), 291-305.

288. *Ibid.*, LXXIV (February 1969), 861-879.

289. *Ibid.*, 862-863, 869, 879, 873.

290. *Journal of American History*, LV (June 1968), 16, 12, 8, 11, 13.

291. In Boorstin, ed., *American Primer*, 671-672.

292. *Chicago Sun-Times*, March 26, 1967, 36.

293. Henry Steele Commager, "Topics: Revolution 1776 and 1789," *New York Times*, July 5, 1969. (See also Commager's letter to the editor,

ibid., April 26, 1969, 36.) In September of 1969 CBS radio stations carried an advertisement sponsored by the American Bar Association. It alluded to Commager's article — without mentioning his name —to make the point that the American Revolution had not turned its back on tradition and that orderly change through law was the American Way.

294. (2 vols.; New York, 1968).

295. See advertisement, *New York Times*, August 4, 1968, E7.

296. Handlin, *History*, II, 651, 639; emphasis added. See also John Morton Blum, *The Promise of America* (Baltimore, 1967), xi: "This inquiry intends to obscure no blemishes, but it does endeavor to rejoice, to describe those patterns that disclose—even for the impatient, perhaps especially for them—the nobility and the power, the mission and the magnificence of the United States."

297. Samuel Eliot Morison, Henry Steele Commager, and William E. Leuchtenburg, *The Growth of the American Republic* (2 vols.; New York, 1969).

298. See above, note 255.

299. Morison, Commager and Leuchtenburg, *Growth*, II, 776, 779. The "hawks" were conservative Republicans and the public, whose opinion as registered in Leuchtenburg's polls showed "as late as the spring of 1967 . . . that a preponderance of opinion favoured strong measures to end the war quickly" (*ibid.*, II, 779).

300. *Ibid.*, II, 779-781.

301. See James P. O'Brien, "The New Left's Early Years," *Radical America*, II (May-June 1968), 23-25; *idem*, "The New Left, 1965-67," *ibid.*, II (September-October 1968), 1-22.

302. Morison, Commager, and Leuchtenburg, *Growth*, II, 782.

303. *Ibid.*, II, 785, 788.

304. *Ibid.*, II, 789.

305. *Ibid.*, II, 789-790.

ACKNOWLEDGMENTS

A few works have influenced my thinking in a general way which is perhaps not adequately reflected by the specific citations below. I am especially indebted to: Michael Paul Rogin, *The Intellectuals and McCarthy: The Radical Specter* (Cambridge, 1967); John Higham, "Beyond Consensus: The Historian as Moral Critic," *American Historical Review*, LXVII (April 1962), 609-625; *idem*, "The Cult of the 'American Consensus': Homogenizing Our History," *Commentary*, XXVII (February 1959), 93-100; Herbert Aptheker, *The Era of McCarthyism* (New York, 1962) [reprint of *History and Reality* (New York, 1955)]; *idem, Laureates of Imperialism* (New York, 1954); Norman Pollack, "Fear of Man: Populism, Authoritarianism, and the Historian," *Agricultural History*, XXXIX (1965), no. 2, 599-67; Christopher Lasch, "The Cultural Cold War: A Short History of the Congress for Cultural Freedom," in Barton J. Bernstein, ed., *Towards a New Past: Dissenting Essays in American History* (New York, 1968), 322-359.

I am indebted to Christopher Z. Hobson, whose criticism has affected my thinking about both the substance and the structure of this paper. Professor Alfred F. Young of the Department of History, Northern Illinois University, has struggled for the freedom of academics over a period of many years and deserves the respect and the gratitude of the entire profession. He has mine. He has provided me with diverse documents concerning past academic freedom controversies; he has also furnished copies of many of the historical writings and public utterances of leading historians which appeared, as did much of the academic freedom material, in newspapers, magazines, pamphlets, and elsewhere during the period since World War II. This ''Young Collection'' has been a rich source of the kind of materials which are essential for such a study as this but which would have been extremely difficult for the researcher working in the late 'sixties to assemble.

ABOUT THE AUTHOR

Jesse Lemisch is an historian in the American Studies Programme at the State University of New York at Buffalo. His other publications include:

Naomi Weisstein, Virginia Blaisdell and Jesse Lemisch. *The Godfathers: Freudians, Marxists, and the Scientific and Political Protection Societies*, (Belladonna Publishing, 884 Elm Street, New Haven, Conn. 06501, 1975).

Jesse Lemisch. "The Papers of a Few Great Black Men and a Few Great White Women", *The Maryland Historian*, VI, No. 1, (Spring 1975) 60-66.

_____. "History, Complete with Historian", *New York Times Book Review*, November 19, 1972, 71.

_____. "The White Oaks, Jack Tar, and the Concept of the 'Inarticulate'", [with John K. Alexander], *William and Mary Quarterly*, 3rd. Series, XXIX, No. 1, (January 1972) 109-134.

_____. "The American Revolution Bicentennial and the Papers of Great White Men: A Preliminary Critique of Current Documentary Publication Programs and Some Alternative Proposals", *AHA Newsletter*, IX, No. 5, (November 1971) 7-21.

_____. "Radical Plot in Boston (1770): A Study in the Use of Evidence", *Harvard Law Review*, LXXXIV, No. 2, (December 1970) 485-504.

_____. "'What's Your Evidence?' Radical Scholarship as Scientific Method and Anti-Authoritarianism, Not 'Relevance'", *New University Conference Papers*, No. 2.

_____. "Listening to the 'Inarticulate': William Widger's Dream and the Loyalties of American Revolutionary Seamen in British Prisons", *Journal of Social History*, III, No. 1, (Fall 1969) 1-29.
Reprinted in:
Thomas N. Guinsburg, ed., *The Dimensions of History*, (Chicago: Rand McNally, 1971).
Blanche W. Cook, Alice K. Harris, Ronald Radosh, eds., *Past Imperfect: Alternative Essays in American History*, (New York: Knopf, 1973).

_____. "If You Gotta Ask, Man, You'll Never Know", *Independent Socialist*, (September 1969).

_____. "Response to Aileen Kraditor", *American Historical Review*, LXXIV, No. 5, (June 1969) 1766-1768.

_____. "Jack Tar in the Streets: Merchant Seamen in the Politics of Revolutionary America", *William and Mary Quarterly*, 3rd. Series, XXV, No. 3, (July 1968) 371-407; also published as "The Radicalism

of the Inarticulate: Merchant Seamen in the Politics of Revolutionary America", in Alfred F. Young, ed., *Dissent: Explorations in the History of American Radicalism*, (DeKalb: Northern Illinois University Press, 1968) 37-82.
Reprinted in:
> William Appleman Williams, ed., *The Shaping of American Diplomacy*, (Chicago: Rand McNally, 1970).
>
> Irwin Unger, ed., *Beyond Liberalism: The New Left Views American History*, (Waltham, Mass.: Xerox, 1971).
>
> Marvin Meyers, J.R. Pole, Thomas Cochran, Charles Dew, and T. Harry Williams, eds., *The Meanings of American History: Interpretations of Events, Ideas, and Institutions*, (Glenview, Ill.: Scott, Foresman, 1971).
>
> Issued in *Bobbs Merrill Reprint Series in American History*, No. H431 (1972).
>
> James M. Banner Jr., Sheldon Hackney, and Barton J. Bernstein, eds., *Selected Readings in American History*, (New York: Harcourt, Brace, Jovanovich, 1973).
>
> John C. Wahlke, ed. [Problems in American Civilization] *The Causes of the American Revolution*, (Lexington, Mass.: D.C. Heath, 3rd ed., 1973).

_____. "What Made Our Revolution", *The New Republic*, May 25, 1968, 25-28.
Reprinted in:
> Blanche W. Cook, Alice K. Harris, Ronald Radosh, eds., *Past Imperfect: Alternative Essays in American History*, (New York: Knopf, 1973).
>
> John C. Wahlke, ed., [Problems in American Civilization] *The Causes of the American Revolution*, (Lexington, Mass.: D.C. Heath, 3rd. ed., 1973).

_____. "The American Revolution Seen From the Bottom Up", in Barton J. Bernstein, ed., *Towards a New Past: Dissenting Essays in American History*, (New York: Pantheon Books, 1968; Vintage paperback, 1969; London: Chatto & Windus, 1970), 3-45.
Reprinted in:
> George Athan Billias, ed., *The American Revolution: How Revolutionary Was It?* (New York: Holt, Rinehart & Winston, 1970).
>
> Richard J. Hooker, ed., *The American Revolution: The Search For Meaning*, (New York: John Wiley, 1970).
>
> Gerald N. Grob and George Athan Billias, eds., *Interpretations of American History: Patterns and Perspectives*, (New York: Free Press, 2nd. ed., 1972).
>
> *Annual Editions: Readings in American History, '73-'74*, (Guilford, Conn.: Dushkin, 1973).

_____. "Who Will Write a Left History of Art While We Are All Putting Our Balls on the Line?", (Boston: New England Free Press, 1968).

_____. "New Left Elitism", *Radical America*, I, (September-October 1967) 43- 53.

_____. "Jack Tar: The Common Seaman" in "The Making of the American Revolution", Edmund S. Morgan, ed. (Part VI of *From*

Subject to Citizen, a junior high school course, (Cambridge, Mass.: Educational Services, Inc., 1966).
Reprinted by:
Dennoyer Geppert, 5235 Ravens Wood Avenue, Chicago, Illinois 60640.

_____. "New York's Petitions and Resolves of December 1765: Liberals Vs. Radicals", *New York Historical Society Quarterly*, XLIX, No. 4, (October 1965) 313-326.

_____. "Who Won the Civil War, Anyway?", *The Nation*, (April 8, 1961).

_____, ed., *Benjamin Franklin: Autobiography and Other Writings*, (New York: New American Library, 1961).

_____, editor and reader. *Benjamin Franklin: Autobiography*, (New York: Folkways Records, 1961).